JONATHAN HOLMES i
He has directed and pro
productions and has ru
currently making a doc
Peace, the book accom
2007. He is Creative A
author of two previous books. He also holds a PhD in
Shakespeare Studies, coordinated the premiere of several
John Donne songs in St Paul's Cathedral in 2005, and is
Senior Lecturer in Drama at Royal Holloway, University
of London.

SCILLA ELWORTHY has been awarded the Niwano
Peace Prize from Japan, and been nominated for the Nobel
Peace Prize three times. She specializes in the effectiveness
of conflict prevention and methods of resolution, and
advises political and military policy-makers. She is founder
of the Oxford Research Group and Peace Direct.

FALLUJAH

Eyewitness testimony from Iraq's besieged city

JONATHAN HOLMES

CONSTABLE • LONDON

Constable & Robinson Ltd
3 The Lanchesters
162 Fulham Palace Road
London W6 9ER
www.constablerobinson.com

First published in the UK by Constable,
an imprint of Constable & Robinson Ltd, 2007

A copy of the British Library Cataloguing in
Publication Data is available from the British Library.

ISBN: 978-1-84529-373-4

Printed and bound in the EU

1 3 5 7 9 10 8 6 4 2

Fallujah has become Iraq, and Iraq now is Fallujah
– Senior Iraqi source

Contents

Acknowledgements

Many people have given of their time, testimony and energy in the creation of both this book and the play it contains. I am deeply grateful to the courageous individuals whose testimony lies at its heart; not only those named in the text, but all those who were unable to go on record for one reason or another: military personnel, Iraqi exiles and former residents of Fallujah; policy-makers and civil servants. In particular I must thank the remarkable figures of Jo Wilding and Dahr Jamail.

More widely, it gives me great pleasure to be able to acknowledge the help and support of Rana al-Aiouby, Naji Haraj, Mohamed Osman, Nitin Sawhney, Lucy Orta, Peter Readman, Fiona Shaw, Nicolas Kent, Anna Linstrum, Alice Bray, Claire Davis, Ellen Mainwood, Sasha Roberts, Suzie Leighton, Sarah Chambers (and others at LCACE), Isabelle Fremeaux, Julia Guest, Cressida Langlands and Polly McLean.

This book, in a real sense, would not have been possible without the efforts of Becky Hardie, and of Nicola Chalmers, whose editorial work made it happen. Special thanks are due to George Monbiot, for permitting me to reprint his article 'War Without Rules'. Most of all I am grateful to Scilla Elworthy, who initiated this whole endeavour and who has supported it throughout.

Jonathan Holmes, Winter 2006

Introduction

This project was born from another. In late 2004 I began work on a documentary film investigating peacemaking, for which I interviewed peacemakers across the globe. In the course of preparing, researching and shooting the film I met many extraordinary people working in extreme circumstances in dangerous locations. I also came to know as friends the equally extraordinary people who, while not themselves in situations of immediate risk, dedicate their lives to supporting those who are.

Principal among the latter were the people at Peace Direct and the Oxford Research Group, both organizations founded by Dr Scilla Elworthy, and both in different ways devoted to finding solutions to conflict. In the summer of 2005, Scilla asked me to become involved in research she was doing into the assault on Fallujah and the suspected war crimes carried out during it. Subsequently, through her agency, I met and spoke to many people whose testimony was so powerful and shocking that Scilla and I began to talk about the possibility of the material becoming a play. Scilla's own research at that time into the situation in Fallujah constitutes the core of her authoritative contextual article in this book.

The first meeting I attended while doing research for the play, organized by the Oxford Research Group, comprised several powerful and highly experienced individuals central to the coalition command and the US/UK presence in the region. They cannot be named, and I am unable to supply any more circumstances of the conversations that took place, except to say that all present impressed me hugely by their sincere commitment to improving the situation within Iraq. My first preconception was shattered; here were senior military men who really cared about the implications of their actions. My second surprise, as an atheist, was to hear religious leaders speaking pragmatically, sanely, and with a thorough grasp of *realpolitik*. Despite being Christians involved in an Islamic country, they followed no prescriptive ecclesiastical line, and displayed extensive knowledge of the culture and traditions of the people with whom they were dealing.

Much of the material garnered from this initial meeting came to be included in the play more or less as it was expressed.[1] The meeting itself led to conversations with other rational and clear-sighted individuals in exile from Fallujah, who also agreed to speak to me on condition of anonymity. I am not a journalist, and had not known quite what a terrible thing it is to speak with people who have to guard their identities because of the impact their statements might have on the lives of others. The responsibility is sobering.

The next step was to talk to those people who were able to go on record with their experiences. Through contacts I had made I was able to speak to Jo Wilding, about whom I had heard already. She had featured in a documentary made by Julia Guest, entitled *A Letter to the Prime Minister,* which had been doing the rounds of independent cinemas in London; I'd managed to borrow a copy on DVD.

Jo is an extraordinary figure. Convinced of the inequity and iniquity of the Blairite stance on Iraq, she had deliberately broken sanctions in order to be brought to

---

1 It can be found in Scene 5.

court and thereby draw attention to the government's damaging anti-Iraq policies. Subsequently she went to Iraq, and to Fallujah. Her accounts of her time there are vivid, passionate and precise in their record of abuse and violation, of a war machine utterly contemptuous of the civilian population – whom they were supposedly there to protect and to liberate. Her writings initially stem from her time in the city in April 2004, though she went there again later with – of all things – a circus. With their rare combination of lucid detail and fierce conviction her journals constitute a rallying cry in the face of corruption on a massive scale. Some of them – the ones most pertinent to the play – are reprinted in this volume, and constitute a personal chronicle of Fallujah to accompany Scilla's objective contextualization.

In a slightly more official capacity, the Canadian journalist Dahr Jamail had been reporting from Iraq for some time. His experiences in Fallujah have provided essential evidence of human rights abuses and derogation of duty on the part of the US military, as well as providing a substantial and often disturbing archive of photographic evidence, all of which can be found at www.dahrjamailiraq.com. Some of his reports, too, are reprinted here. Dahr's accounts include interviews he himself carried out with Fallujan citizens, which in turn became valuable for the play.

One aspect of the suppression of dissent in Fallujah was the blanket ban imposed by the US military on reporting from the city. Consequently, if it hadn't been for the heroism of people like Dahr and Jo, very few first-hand accounts would have reached Western media outlets. Nevertheless, through interviewing and recording the testimony of those who have been there – soldiers, doctors, aid workers, civilian exiles – it is possible to build an eyewitness picture of the disturbing situation within the city. By cross-referencing accounts and juxtaposing them with photographic, video and surveillance evidence it is possible to see just what life has been like in the city, and just how appallingly the occupying forces have behaved over the past three years. The essay in this volume on Fallujah and the Geneva Conventions makes clear just how bad the situation is: the Americans have violated seventy separate articles of the conventions, repeatedly and with impunity.

The general state of affairs in Iraq has been catalogued in more poetic fashion by the American writer Eliot Weinberger in a now-iconic piece, *What I Heard About Iraq* (for the *London Review of Books*, January 2005). The piece is, in Borgesian fashion, halfway between an essay and a poem, and uses the disinformation and lies of the Bush administration in counterpoint with the reality of life on the ground in Iraq to create a heartbreaking sequence of snapshots of a tragedy. The full text is readily available in print and on the web, and its simplicity and power were a significant inspiration for the play; indeed, its full text has been performed itself as a protest piece in cities around the world. Its inclusion in this book gives a unique perspective on the wider situation in the country; a wide-angle response to add to Jo's close-ups.

In the course of making *Perpetual Peace*, my film about peacemaking, I had met and interviewed George Monbiot. His piece on chemical weapons usage in Fallujah was one of the first to make public this particularly disgraceful episode in the history of the US Armed Forces, and I am grateful to him for allowing it to be included in this volume.

There are two principal atrocities in Fallujah. The first is the criminal behaviour of American troops. The second is the failure of the West to condemn that behaviour. The prevention of news broadcasts from the city undoubtedly played a major part in this lack of condemnation, and additional reasons can be found in the reluctance of European governments, especially that of the UK, to criticize the Bush administration's actions for fear of covert reprisal.

It is too late fully to remedy the situation in Fallujah: the damage has been done, and it is extremely doubtful whether the inhabitants will ever have meaningful redress. There remains only the opportunity to publicize the disgrace, and to condemn it noisily. As the muted outcry over the massacre of twenty-four civilians by US forces in Haditha in November 2005 (which went unreported until May 2006) has shown, governments cannot ignore such a reaction entirely. To quote Brigadier General Mark Kimmitt in an alternative context, the responses to situations such as this need to be 'methodical, precise and overwhelming'. Methodical preparation, precise expression and overwhelming commitment to peaceful and intelligent opposition can begin to make an effect, but it needs to be sustained, coherent and visible.

As a culture it seems that we have lost our sense of collective perseverance; one march will not change things, even if a million people take part, but ten years of marches will. It is a sign of how successful structures of power have been in instilling ideologies of immediate gratification and political apathy that so many prominent intellectuals have admitted defeat so readily. One cannot learn a language in a day, and one cannot change government policy overnight; it is madness to assume either, and yet we continue to be disillusioned when the latter does not occur.

This book contains five responses to the siege of Fallujah: Scilla's essay discussing the context for the attack and its repercussions; eyewitness testimony; George's piece about illegal weapons usage; an article by me detailing the rape of the Geneva Conventions by the US military; and a play composed of testimony from those involved. The book, I suppose, could be subtitled *Voices from Fallujah;* the result is a glimpse, a brief aperture into the lives of Fallujan citizens and the horrific situation they have had to endure. It is, in a way, a textual equivalent of a photojournalism exhibition.

All the responses here are, essentially, acts of witnessing. Whether informed responses to the wider situation, direct testimony from those in the thick of it, or a mode of communication that allows groups of spectators to listen to otherwise unheard voices, everything in this book originates from a powerful desire to bear witness. For me, a collective act of witnessing is what the theatre necessarily involves, one that is inescapably ethical, as it requires us to take responsibility for our response to what we experience. We do the same when we engage as readers, and it is in this witnessing that art can be a vehicle for resistance to oppression.

Jonathan Holmes, 2007

Timeline of Principal Events in the Siege of Fallujah

2003

23 April: city entered by US troops. Initial headquarters established at former Ba'ath Party offices.

26–27 April: 82nd Airborne Division moves their base to al-Qa'id primary school.

28 April: 400 people demonstrate peacefully against the occupation of the school. US troops open fire killing 20 and wounding 85.

29–30 April: larger demonstrations in the city.

May: Iraqi police disbanded, all borders to the west of Iraq left open, all Iraqis forbidden to carry arms.

2004

6 January: two French nationals working for US companies are killed and a third is wounded in a drive-by shooting in the city. A US Apache helicopter is shot down west of Fallujah near al-Habbaniya.

9 January: nine US soldiers are killed when their Blackhawk helicopter is shot down in the city.

13 January: four civilian protesters, including an elderly woman, are killed and five others are seriously wounded by US forces.

13 February: the head of US Central Command in the Middle East, General John Abizaid, escapes an assassination attempt (an attack by rocket-propelled grenades) in Fallujah.

20 March: the 1st Marines Expeditionary Force10 (IMEF), commanded by Lieutenant General Conway, take over responsibility in al-Anbar province from the army's 82nd Airborne Division commanded by Major General Swannack.

Early April: Fallujah is closed off and curfews are imposed.

5 April: the launch of Operation Vigilant Resolve. Hospitals and mosques are targeted and residents are blocked from exiting the city.

10 April: casualties number 500 Iraqi wounded, 300 Iraqi dead and 5 US dead. Fighting continues for the rest of April.

29 April: US troops withdraw to the city circumference. Insurgents consolidate their position in the city centre. Bombardments of the city continue throughout the summer.

12 September: outgoing Lieutenant General Conway says the April assault was an 'overly aggressive mistake'.

7 November: once again all exits and roads to the city are sealed off. Fallujah is under total siege.

8 November: Operation Phantom Fury is launched. Chemical weapons are used.

December: by this stage, 80 per cent of the city's population are refugees.

2005

Spring: people slowly begin to return to the city, which is without water, electricity or sanitation. Seventy per cent of the city has been bombed to the ground.

Background: the situation in Fallujah

Scilla Elworthy

Dr Scilla Elworthy founded the Oxford Research Group (ORG) in 1982 and was Executive Director until December 2003. The Group established a reputation for powerful independent research into military decision-making, resulting in its ability to organize meetings between the most senior policy-makers and their critics in all the nuclear nations, including China. It is for this work that she was awarded the Niwano Peace Prize in 2003 and has been nominated three times for the Nobel Peace Prize. In 2003 she founded Peace Direct, which grew out of the ORG's conflict-prevention work and which was named 'Best New Charity' at the Charity Times Awards in 2005.

This article is based on the case study of Fallujah undertaken in 2005 and critiqued at a seminar in July 2005 by journalists, church leaders, NGOs and senior British and US military.

Fallujah (Arabic: ﺔﺟﻮﻟﻒ; sometimes transliterated as **Falluja**) is a city of between 350,000 and 500,000 inhabitants (about the size of Edinburgh) in the Iraqi province of al-Anbar, located roughly 69km (43 miles) west of Baghdad on the east bank of the Euphrates. Within Iraq, it is known as the 'city of mosques' for the 200 or more mosques found in the city and surrounding villages; as well as places of worship, these mosques were schools of

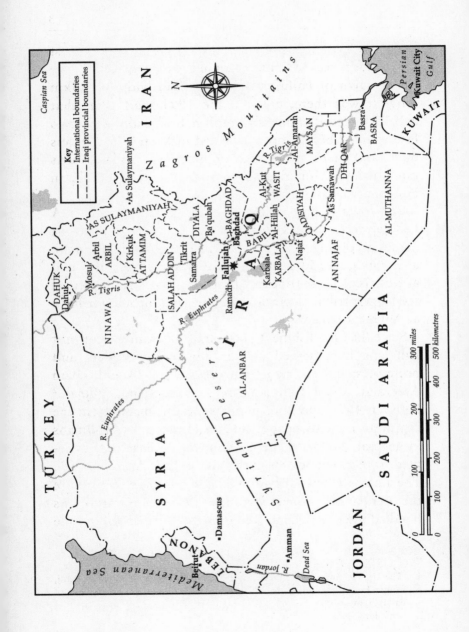

language, Islamic history and law. It is one of the most important places of Sunni Islam in the region.

The town of Fallujah measures 3km wide by 3.5km long. It was there, early in the 1991 Gulf War, that a British jet intending to bomb a bridge dropped two laser-guided bombs on a crowded market; 276 civilians died[1] and many more were injured. Yet Fallujah was not hostile to American-led efforts to remove Saddam Hussein from power.

The town is part of the so-called 'Sunni Triangle'. A Fallujah resident says 'You will find people with their last names according to their tribes, like: al-Aisawi, al-Janabi, al-Zouba'i, al-Mohammadi, al-Alwani, al-Jumaily, and al-Kubaisy.' These tribes are branches of al-Dulaim, one of the biggest tribal federations in Iraq, and the main tribe in al-Anbar province.

Since the establishment of the Iraqi state, many eminent Fallujans have served as ministers, army leaders and professors; indeed, two Iraqi presidents – Abdul Salam Aref and Abdul Rahman Aref – were from Fallujah.[2] Between 1970 and 2003 fundamentalist imams from the city were imprisoned by Saddam Hussein, but Fallujans in general supported the government because they benefited from developments in education, housing and health. The imams (sheikhs) had a relatively minor role before the occupation as the government and its civil institutions handled internal affairs. But after the occupation and the

---

1 'The US Treatment of Fallujah: the Fallujan View', report by Naji Haraj, former Iraqi diplomat at the UN in Geneva (1999–2003) and resident of Fallujah, May 2005.
2 Naji Haraj, *ibid.*

dissolving of most institutions, the vacuum that opened up was filled by tribal and religious sheikhs.

The local power structure was described as 'the product of alliances between fiercely insular tribal clans, a growing Islamic movement and former Ba'ath Party businessmen and intelligence officers, who have helped bankroll the insurgency and plot some of its more sophisticated attacks'.[3] But Dr Muhammad al-Hamadani, a Fallujan resident, told Aljazeera.net on 19 July 2004 that he had no knowledge about any non-Iraqi fighters in the town. 'As a Fallujah citizen, and head of the Fallujah Scientific Forum, I can tell you that I have never seen or heard anything about non-Iraqi fighters in Fallujah. We hear about al-Zarqawi in the media, but have never seen or felt his presence or any of his followers in Fallujah.'

The invasion of March/April 2003

Owing to its social and religious structures, there was no looting or civil disorder in Fallujah during the initial invasion, as there was in Baghdad and elsewhere. Local leaders selected a governing council which took responsibility for keeping security and running the main services in the city. When US forces entered the town on 23 April 2003, they chose the former headquarters of the Ba'ath Party, in the outskirts of the city, as their HQ.

On 26 and 27 April 2003, some of the American troops from the 82nd Airborne moved from their headquarters to the al-Qa'id primary school in Nzal residential area and

---

3   Alissa J Rubin, *Los Angeles Times*, 7 April 2004.

converted it to a military base. Their reasons for doing this is not known, nor is it clear whether they explained them to local leaders. On 28 April, about 400 people – most of them school students, relatives and teachers – demonstrated near the main American base and then moved to the front of the school to express their opposition to its takeover.

Reports indicate that this was a peaceful demonstration, to try to make the US forces leave the school they had occupied, by people wanting their children to be able to continue attending school. Prior to that there had been no resistance to the occupation. When the demonstration came close to the outer wall of the school, the US army opened fire. A total of twenty people were killed, three of them children under the age of ten, with more than eighty-five wounded.[4] There are first-hand reports from British and Iraqi sources of people being shot while recovering bodies, and ambulance crews also came under fire. Thousands of people joined a second and third demonstration on 29 and 30 April, condemning the US acts and demanding the immediate withdrawal of American forces.

From a US perspective, the demonstrations may have seemed part of a pattern of unrest after the invasion, in a city that was seen as a former Ba'athist stronghold. A particularly robust approach possibly appeared necessary as an example to Sunni resistance in other parts of the triangle.

---

4 Associated Press International 29 April 2004 reports confirmed by US soldiers. Jassim Awad, whose fifteen-year-old brother was wounded, told the *New York Times*: 'It took me three hours to get him out. I even walked with a white flag so they knew we only wanted to get our bodies and injured out, and they just said no, no, no!.'

From a Fallujan perspective, militancy intensified as house arrests increased and people were disappearing into Abu Ghraib prison, some 30km away. The detention and treatment of the Abu Ghraib prisoners, many of them from Fallujah, became a significant factor in the unrest in the city. House raids seem to exhibit a general pattern, summarized in a February 2004 report by the International Committee of the Red Cross, based on its investigation of reported incidents:

> Arresting authorities entered houses usually after dark, breaking down doors, waking up residents roughly, yelling orders, forcing family members into one room under military guard while searching the rest of the house and further breaking doors, cabinets, and other property. They arrested suspects, tying their hands in the back with flexicuffs, hooding them, and taking them away. Sometimes they arrested all adult males in the house, including elderly, handicapped, or sick people. Treatment often included pushing people around, insulting, taking aim with rifles, punching and kicking, and striking with rifles. Individuals were often led away in whatever they happened to be wearing at the time of arrest – sometimes pyjamas or underwear... In many cases personal belongings were seized during the arrest with no receipt given... In almost all incidents documented by the ICRC, arresting authorities provided no information about who they were nor where their base was located, nor did they explain the cause of arrest. Similarly, they rarely informed the arrestee or his family where he was being taken or for how long, resulting in the defacto disappearance of the arrestee for weeks or even months until contact was finally made.

In May 2003 Iraqi military personnel, police and security services were disbanded, with their weapons, 'and for ten months Iraq's borders were left open for anyone to come in without even a visa or a passport'.[5] The mass dismissal of government and army personnel disproportionately affected Sunnis: 'De-Baathification' measures have fallen most heavily on Sunnis, including many who are recognized as leaders or prominent individuals in their communities.

Some negotiation was tried, with the broad aim of splitting the hard core from the broader Sunni community. The problem, according to an experienced British diplomat, was that US military tactics used during the invasion and in seeking to secure the country had killed and injured many Iraqis, particularly in Sunni areas, where the resistance was strongest. This reinforced the perception among the Sunni community of the coalition as a hostile invader no better than the regime it had swept away. The post-invasion chaos, failure to restore and improve services, abuses at Abu Ghraib, US administration rhetoric and its wider Middle East policies, particularly on Israel, amplified in the Arab press and satellite television (Al-Jazeera, Al-Arabiya) added to the hostility.

The city became militant and resistance grew from the time of the shootings at the school; several informed observers say that the deaths led directly to the killing of four American contractors a year later. Fallujans became suspicious of any foreigner entering their city, and the US gradually lost control of most of the city.

---

5 Ghazi al-Yawer, Iraq's first interim president, quoted in 'Vicious Circle: The Dynamics of Occupation and Resistance in Iraq' by Carl Conetta, Project on Defense Alternatives, May 2005.

The deaths of US contractors, 31 March 2004

On 31 March 2004 four US contract employees were killed in Fallujah, their mutilated corpses dragged through the city and hung on the bridge. Shock waves reverberated through US media, and US military officials vowed a major response.

From that point, Fallujah was sealed off by US troops and off-limits to Westerners. On 5 April Associated Press reported that US troops closed off entrances to Fallujah with earth barricades, ahead of the planned operation code-named 'Vigilant Resolve'. Iraqi police in the city visited mosques, dropping off Arabic leaflets from the US military, telling residents that there was a daily 7pm to 6am curfew. It ordered them not to congregate in groups or carry weapons, even if licensed. It instructed people that if US forces entered their homes, they should gather in one room and if they wanted to talk to the troops to have their hands up.

The *Los Angeles Times* reported that 'Working through the cold and windy desert night, under a large moon, Marines set up camps for detainees and residents who might flee... Before dawn, several Marine positions on the fringes of town were hit by mortar rounds and rocket-propelled grenade fire; one Marine was reported killed... At daylight, Marines in armored Humvees began distributing leaflets asking residents to stay in their homes and help identify insurgents and those responsible for last week's killings. They also took over the local radio station and used bullhorns to get the message out. "We are going to stop the anarchy inside this city," one announcement said; another asserted that insurgents were violating the

peaceful tenets of Islam ... Marines said they had no plans
to conduct random door-to-door searches; they instead
intended to work from a list of addresses where intelligence
suggested suspects might be hiding and weapons might be
stored. Marine officials said the cordon of Fallujah will
last as long as it takes to clear the town of weapons caches
and a long list of suspected insurgents.'"

There were indications on 2 April that anti-coalition
forces were preparing for a fight in the city. One source
with close ties to the anti-US resistance forces told United
Press International (UPI) that fighters from throughout
the region had begun slipping into Fallujah in preparation
for what they assumed would be a significant US military
operation. One such fighter – who normally operates in
Baghdad – told UPI he would leave immediately to join a
cell in Fallujah and that fighters were also entering the city
from the neighbouring city of Ramadi. 'Fallujah is where
we fight the invaders,' a source familiar with the work-
ings of the resistance told UPI through an intermediary.
'Ramadi is where our leadership and operations are based.
They are moving (resources) into Fallujah for this fight.
We will make Fallujah the graveyard of America.'⁶

Seen from the perspective of US leadership, news of
such resistance build-up must have been threatening, and
it provided the basis for a substantial military operation
to attempt to destroy the opposition concentrated in one
city. US military commanders would have been in receipt
of reports such as the following: 'It is part of the ritual
of manhood for some people now, that you have to have

6 The Iraq Body Count Fallujah Archive is derived from nearly 300 selected
   news stories on the April 2004 siege of Fallujah.

killed an American soldier to be respected. The guys who killed the guards disappeared straight away: teenagers attacked the bodies afterwards to try and say, "I am a man". Nobody will hand them over to the Americans, though: we will just give them a talking to and tell them "not again".' [7]

The US assault on Fallujah, 5/6 April 2004

On 5 April Operation Vigilant Resolve was launched. US warplanes firing rockets destroyed four houses in Fallujah. A doctor said twenty-six Iraqis, including women and children, were killed and thirty wounded in the strike.[8] Marines waged a fierce battle for hours with gunmen holed up in Jolan, a residential neighbourhood of Fallujah. The military used an AC-130 gunship to lay down a barrage of fire against the gunmen, and commanders said Marines were holding an area several blocks deep inside the city. At least two Marines were wounded. Heavy fighting also occurred between Marines entrenched in the desert and guerrillas firing from houses on Fallujah's northeast outskirts. The only operating hospital in Fallujah was hit by US tank and missile fire overnight.[9]

Channel 4 News reported[10] that Fallujans were prevented from leaving the city, and that US forces had closed bridges

---

7 Colin Freeman, *Daily Telegraph*, 4 April 2004.
8 API 6 April 2004, confirmed by the *Guardian*.
9 Dr Kamal Al Anni, head surgeon of the main hospital, was shown having to operate in makeshift quarters in a film shown on Channel 4 News on 27 May 2004.
10 'Fallujah Forensics' Tara Sutton for Guardian Films, broadcast 27 May 2004.

leading to the hospital. Brigadier General Mark Kimmitt in a press conference dismissed this as propaganda, famously instructing the attending media to 'change the channel'.

Hospital sources said at least forty-five Iraqis were killed and ninety injured in attacks the next day;[11] among the casualties was a family sitting in a car parked behind the Abd al-Aziz al-Samarai mosque when it was bombed by a US airplane. American forces initially said those killed in the attack on the mosque were fighters taking refuge. But a Marine officer later admitted that US forces had failed to find any bodies. 'When we hit that building I thought we had killed all the bad guys, but when we went in they didn't find any bad guys in the building,' Lieutenant Colonel Brennan Byrne told reporters.

From the US perspective it appeared that several mosques were being used by the insurgents as strongholds from which to fire at Marines. Outside one particular mosque the Marines apparently allowed Fallujans to come in to take the insurgent wounded away. But instead, people with rocket-propelled grenades jumped out of the ambulances and started fighting with the Marines. The Marines called in air power. A helicopter dropped a Hellfire missile and then an F-16 dropped a laser-guided bomb on the outside of the mosque. But when the Marines examined the mosque door-to-door and floor-to-floor, they found no bodies, nor did they find the kind of blood and guts one would expect if people had died. 'The Marines were quite willing to kill everybody in the mosque because they were insurgents. They had been firing at people, at Marines. And as the lieutenant colonel who ordered the strikes said,

---

11 API 7 April 2004.

this was no longer a house of worship; this was a military target.' [12]

'Some of the fighters are young guys, the equivalent of dope peddlers, who do this for money. Others are holy warriors willing to die for a cause,' said Captain Will Dickens, another company commander whose troops were fired on repeatedly. 'The die-hard [suicide fighters] just stand up in the open, fire from the hip and stay there until they kill or are killed.'[13]

The US perspective was summed up by Lieutenant Colonel Brennan Byrne: 'This is not retribution. This is not vendetta. This is about making the city liveable so people don't have to live in fear of the thugs who have taken over the city...This city has long been a haven for smugglers and bandits, a dumping ground for foreign fighters and bad guys. No one ever took the time to clean it out properly.' The Marines were now fighting street by street, and Patrick Graham of the *Observer* reported talking to US soldiers who were terrified. Channel 4 News reported US forces using sniper fire at civilians stepping out of their homes, and interviewed Dr Salam al-Aoudi, who treated sniper wounds.[14]

From the Fallujan perspective the defence of their city was paramount against an invasion using overwhelming firepower. They were outraged at the shelling of their only operating hospital – not only their only source of emergency medical help but also the only source of figures on numbers of Iraqis killed and injured – and by the reported use of cluster bombs and missiles against civilians. Asso-

---

12 PBS Radio, Gwen Ifill and Tony Perry, 7 April 2004.
13 Pamela Constable, *Washington Post*, 7 April 2004.
14 Film by Tara Sutton, 27 May 2004.

ciated Press reported that US warplanes opened fire on groups of Iraqis in the street. On 9 and 10 April fierce confrontations left over 300 dead and 500 wounded.

April 2004: stalemate

The US military offered a cease-fire deal after Iraqi politicians, decrying 'collective punishment' meted out to people in Fallujah, demanded a halt to the fighting. The aim was to allow peace talks between Iraqi officials and insurgents, with no US participation. Afterwards, Hachim al-Hasani, a representative of the US-appointed Iraqi Governing Council who led the delegation, said he was 'optimistic' about the talks. 'Fallujans want to return to peace and normal life. They are willing to take steps in that direction and the same is true of the coalition forces,' he said. The leaders of the Fallujan insurgency wanted the US Marines to withdraw – at least partially. They also wanted to deploy a locally recruited police force. Iraqi mediators said the two sides had agreed in principle to give ground on some of their demands.

On 17 April Associated Press reported that 'Unable to advance farther into the city, an army psychological operations team hopes a mix of heavy metal and insults shouted in Arabic – including, "You shoot like a goat herder" – will draw gunmen to step forward and attack. At night, the psychological operations unit attached to the Marine battalion here sends out messages from a loud-speaker mounted on an armored Humvee. On Thursday night, the crew and its Arabic-language interpreter taunted fighters, saying, "May all the ambulances in Fallujah have

enough fuel to pick up the bodies of the mujahadeen."
The message was specially timed for an attack moments
later by an AC-130 gunship that pounded targets in the
city. Later, the team blasted Jimi Hendrix and other rock
music, and afterward some sound effects like babies crying,
men screaming, a symphony of cats and barking dogs and
piercing screeches. They were unable to draw any gunmen
to fight, and seemed disappointed.'

By this time it was reported that the offensive had killed
five Marines and more than 600 Iraqis, mostly civilians,
according to hospital sources.

For Iraqis, as reported by *New York Times* correspondent Edward Wong on 22 April, Fallujah had become 'a
galvanizing battle, a symbol around which many Iraqis
rally their anticolonial sentiments'. He interviewed 'the
kind of middle-class Iraqis that Americans are relying on
to help them rebuild the country, with livelihoods already
rooted in the principles of free-market capitalism. Yet their
sense of kinship with Iraqis in Fallujah, Najaf and elsewhere runs deeper than any pull toward abstract notions
of democracy offered by the Americans – notions that to
them appear increasingly hypocritical given the reliance
of the occupiers on overwhelming force as a means to an
end.'

On 22 April[15] senior US military officers estimated
there were in Fallujah about 2,000 hard-core insurgents,
including about 200 foreign fighters, mainly from Syria
and Yemen; former members of the Iraqi Special Repub-
lican Guard and security services; Islamic fighters; and
former members of the Fedayeen militia. On 28 April Ali

---

15 Eric Schmitt, *New York Times*, 22 April 2004.

Allawi, the Iraqi Defence Minister, said that a second unit of the Iraqi armed forces had mutinied at Fallujah after being involved in heavy fighting with insurgents. 'Part of the 36th battalion of the paramilitary Iraqi Civil Defence Corps revolted last week after the unit had been fighting in the besieged city for eleven days. At the start of the siege of Fallujah three weeks ago, one of the five battalions of the newly formed Iraqi army refused to go to the city because many of its soldiers were not prepared to fight fellow Iraqis.'[16]

After the huge numbers of casualties, on 29 April the US agreed to withdraw to the circumference of Fallujah, the centre of which then became a stronghold for insurgents. US forces handed control to an Iraqi militia force – the Fallujah Brigade – under General Jasim Mohammed al-Mohammadi, composed mainly of native Fallujans. Lieutenant General Conway, commander of the 1st Marines Expeditionary Force, told a news conference on 1 May that they were banking on the Iraqi force to douse the resistance in the city.

In July Fallujans began staging sit-ins to demand compensation for property destroyed during the April US military offensive. Carrying banners reading: 'Rebuild our houses from our oil revenues', demonstrators acknowledged that some aid has reached the town, but they told Al-Jazeera's correspondent it is 'nothing in comparison to the cost of the damage already inflicted by US warplanes'.[17]

Throughout the summer and autumn the US military launched air strikes on the city, often on residential areas,

---

16 Patrick Cockburn, *Independent*, 29 April 2004.
17 Al-Jazeera, 19 July 2004.

often killing civilians. US forces claimed that these were targeted, intelligence-based strikes against houses used by the group of Abu Musab al-Zarqawi, an insurgency leader linked to al Qaida. US Marines also engaged in firefights on a daily and nightly basis along the perimeter of the city. 'Fallujah medical sources say their hospital wards are being filled with dead and wounded women and children. Fallujah hospital director Dr al-Isawi called on a delegation from the interim Iraqi government to investigate the nature of the casualties... "I have nine children in the children's [ward] from the bombing," he said. "Every day we receive women, children and elderly people and I confirm that casualties, at least all those I have received at the hospital, were civilians," he added.' [18]

From the Fallujan perspective they were being punished not only for the deaths of the contractors but for 'being the symbol of an uprising that had shaken the US occupation of Iraq to the core. The majority of Iraqis, whether Shiite or Sunni, are uniting around a common demand – that the American military get out of their country. The entry of thousands of Shiite fighters into active resistance on 4 April, alongside the long running guerrilla war being fought in predominantly Sunni areas, has forced US and allied forces to retreat inside fortress compounds in many parts of the country.' [19]

'On 12 September, at his change-of-command ceremony, the outgoing Marine Lieutenant General James Conway gave tragic voice to what thousands of servicemen throughout Iraq have believed for months. He

---

18 Naji Haraj, *ibid*.
19 Naji Haraj, *ibid*.

announced that the April assault on Fallujah had been an overly aggressive mistake.'[20] Another Marine commander said the Fallujah Brigade, the local force given control of the town while Marines pulled back, had turned out to be a 'fiasco'. Marine officers said assault rifles, vehicles and radios given to the Brigade by American forces ended up in the hands of insurgents.[21]

November 2004: Operation 'Phantom Fury'

The US aim by November 2004 was to subdue the city by force. US troops closed all roads in the area and put the city under total siege. On 7 November the Iraq interim government declared a sixty-day state of emergency in preparation for the assault, as insurgents carried out several car bomb attacks in the Fallujah area which killed Iraqi army and police, US soldiers and Iraqi civilians. The next day Prime Minister Iyad Allawi publicly authorized an offensive in Fallujah and Ramadi to 'liberate the people' and 'clean Fallujah from the terrorists'. He said he made this move after all peaceful means to solve the problem had proved ineffective.

On 8 November US Marines and the Iraqi 36th Commando Battalion secured two bridges across the Euphrates, seized a hospital on the outskirts of the city and arrested about fifty men in the hospital. About half the arrested men were later released. A hospital doctor reported that fifteen Iraqis were killed and twenty wounded during

20 David Morris, Salon.com, 16 September 2004.
21 'General criticises Fallujah strategy' News.Telegraph, Toby Harnden in Baghdad, filed 14 September 2004.

the overnight incursions. The *Economist* (13 November 2004) said that the reason for early capture of the hospital was because it was 'the source of damaging reports, last time round, that hundreds of civilians had been killed'.

The Study Centre for Human Rights and Democracy (SCHRD), in its report to the UN Secretary General, records the forces 'tying up doctors and beating them with their shoes. Patients were arrested and deprived of treatment. The only other clinic was hit twice by US missiles and all its medicines and equipment destroyed.' Dr Sami al-Jumaili, who was working in the clinic, says the bombs took the lives of fifteen medics, four nurses and thirty-five patients. Whether the clinic was targeted or destroyed accidentally, the effect was the same: to eliminate many of Fallujah's doctors from the war zone. As Dr al-Jumaili told the *Independent* on 14 November: 'There is not a single surgeon in Fallujah.' When fighting moved to Mosul, a similar tactic was used: on entering the city, US and Iraqi forces immediately seized control of the al-Zaharawi hospital.[22]

By nightfall on 9 November, US troops had reached the heart of the city. US military officials stated that up to 6,000 insurgents were believed to be in the city, but they did not appear to be well organized, and fought in small groups, of three to twenty-five. Many insurgents were believed to have slipped away amid widespread reports that the US offensive was coming.

Reports by the *Washington Post* suggest that US armed forces used white phosphorous (WP) grenades and/or artillery shells, creating walls of fire in the city. White phospho-

---

22 Naomi Klein, letter to US acting Ambassador to London, 4 December 2004.

rous cannot be extinguished by water. Doctors working inside Fallujah reported seeing melted corpses of suspected insurgents. The use of WP ammunition was confirmed by various independent sources, including US troops who had suffered WP burns caused by 'friendly fire'.

On 13 November a US Marine was videotaped shooting a wounded, unarmed alleged insurgent to death in a mosque. The incident created controversy throughout the world. The Geneva Convention Relative to the Protection of Civilian Persons in Time of War, which was adopted in 1949 and which entered into force in 1950, dictates that 'persons taking no active part in the hostilities, including members of armed forces who have laid down their arms and those placed *hors de combat* by sickness, wounds, detention, or any other cause, shall in all circumstances be treated humanely,' and that they 'shall be protected especially against all acts of violence or threats thereof and against insults and public curiosity'. The incident further inflamed Iraqi and world opinion when, six months later, the soldier was later found not guilty.

From the US perspective, every person remaining in Fallujah was suspect. Some of the tactics used by the insurgents included wearing civilian clothing while attacking, playing dead and attacking, surrendering and attacking, rigging dead or wounded people with bombs, and other acts. In the 13 November incident mentioned above, the US Marine apparently believed the insurgent was playing dead.

'The enemy can dress as a woman, the enemy can be faking to be dead,' said one company commander to his Marines before entering the heart of the city. 'So shoot everything that moves and everything that doesn't move.'[23] When Marines asked a gunnery sergeant for clarification, he told his men if they saw any military-aged males on the street 'Drop 'em'. The night before the assault began, the order apparently came down that troops could shoot any male on the street between the ages of fifteen and fifty if they were viewed as a security threat, regardless of whether or not they had a weapon. Other rules of engagement appear to have been modified. US solders were reported to be authorized to kill injured fighters by the so-called 'double-tap': two bullets in a body when coming across wounded fighters on the ground.[24] This would mean that soldiers were authorized to shoot until they became confident that the wounded person was dead.

On 14 November Associated Press reported that thirty-eight US Marines had been killed and 275 wounded during the Fallujah offensive. SCHRD reported that on 13 November medical staff opened another clinic, but US jets destroyed it, killing everyone including patients, doctors and nurses. 'The sole private hospital in Fallujah was destroyed and its equipment looted by Iraqi National Guard. US forces arrested many civilians and forced men and youth to work cleaning the city to erase evidence. Many witnessed group killings of unarmed civilians arrested in houses and mosques, some shot with hands tied behind their backs, a man with four children found shot in the head. Evidence of cluster bombs being used in residential

---

23 Al-Jazeera (9 December 2004, 7:58 GMT) reporting an un-embedded photographer, who did not wish to identify his unit, which carried out some of the most dangerous missions on the frontlines of the Fallujah battle.
24 Al-Jazeera, *ibid.*

areas of Fallujah, and eyewitnesses also confirmed that US tanks were used to crush dead bodies, as well as living wounded. US soldiers did not allow anyone to take away the bodies; embedded journalists refrained from photographing those shot in the head or any other evidence of deliberate killing of civilians.'

After the November 2004 attack

SCHRD reported thousands of casualties, saying that as late as 25 and 26 December the emergency teams of Fallujah hospital removed 700 bodies from only six (out of twenty-eight) residential quarters, including 504 children and women and the rest old and middle-aged people – all Iraqis. Many bodies appeared to have been burned with chemicals. US forces announced that 1,200 bodies were kept in a refrigerated store.

Residents were allowed to return to the city in mid-December after undergoing biometric identification, provided they wore their ID cards all the time. Only 10 per cent of the pre-offensive inhabitants had returned as of mid-January 2005, and only 30 per cent as of the end of March 2005.[25] According to the official estimate 'almost 36,000 houses have been demolished, 9,000 shops, sixty-five mosques, sixty schools, the very valuable heritage library and most of the government offices. The American forces destroyed one of the two bridges in the city, both train stations, the two electricity stations, and three

25 www.voanews.com/english/2005-03-31-voa6.cfm

water treatment plants. It also blew up the whole sanitation system and the communication network.'[26]

In a Defense Department Briefing, *Progress of Reconstruction Work in Iraq; Plans For Reconstruction in Fallujah*, on 19 November, Bill Taylor, State Department Iraq Reconstruction Management Office, said that the money available for reconstruction in Fallujah 'could get into the order of a hundred million dollars or so'. However, very little of that money had been spent six months later.

Dr Fawzi, an engineer who owns a cement factory in Fallujah, said in May 2005 that the southern districts of the city remained closed, and only 10 per cent of the buildings and homes destroyed had been rebuilt – by the residents themselves. Fawzi was involved in negotiating compensation for residents of the city, and presented a figure of $600 million to the US military, which agreed to pay the amount. But the Iraqi government did not agree. In the same report[27] Dr Abraham Aziz said that only 10 per cent of the promised compensation had been paid out by June 2005, and added that the health situation was 'horrible, we are now having cholera outbreaks'.

Tests on drinking water performed by SCHRD in May 2005 found that there was no potable water available inside Fallujah. 'Everybody knows this, and this is why we are making announcements for people to boil their water for ten minutes,' Mohammed Abdulla, director of SCHRD, told reporter Dahr Jamail in May 2005. According to him, two-thirds of the city lacked electricity because so many electrical wires had been cut, and the only reconstruction

26 Statement by Engineer Hafid al-Dulaimy, chairman of Fallujah Compensation Committee on 23 March 2005.
27 The Failed Siege of Fallujah, Dahr Jamail, *Asia Times*, 3 June 2005.

occurring was that being carried out by the residents of Fallujah, with no outside help. 'There is little financial aid coming from the government, if any at all.'[28]

SCHRD reported that on 27 December 2004 some 350,000 refugees were living in al-Saqlawiya, al-Habbaniya tourist city and camp, al-A'meriya complex, al-Khaldiyah, al-Karma and Khan Dhari, while others went to al-Anbar province and Baghdad. In al-Karma and al-A'meriya complex the density was twenty-five to thirty people in one flat. Monthly quotas of foodstuffs (from the Trade Ministry) were withdrawn from Fallujah residents for September, October and November, meaning that prices rose sharply. Refugees were living in garages and stores and were seriously short of medical services – diseases such as diarrhoea, scabies and asthma spread. Eyewitnesses said that returnees to al-Andalus residential area found their houses intact, but when they went back three days later their houses had been destroyed; apparently US forces were making a film showing their performance and bombarded several areas already under their control, destroying empty houses and setting ablaze twenty houses in al-Shurta area. Compensation of $4,000 was being offered, even though the houses cost no less than $50,000 not including furniture.

As of June 2005 Fallujans said that approximately 100,000 people were still refugees, unable to return to their homes, many of which no longer exist.[29] 'Roughly 60 per cent of the houses and buildings inside the city sustained enough damage to make them inhabitable. Most

28 *Ibid.*
29 Naji Haraj, *ibid.*

people continue to live in tents, or amid the rubble of their homes.'[30]

Nearly a year later, in May 2006, according to the NGO Coordination Committee, Iraq, and the Monitoring Net of Human Rights in Iraq:

- more than two-thirds of the original evacuee population of Fallujah have now returned to the city. The remaining third have not returned, either because they found their homes and/or neighbourhoods completely destroyed, or because they expected future offensives and preferred to settle in other places
- in the second half of 2005 Fallujah became a host city for Internally Displaced Persons from other cities in Iraq which had been afflicted by military operations (such as Heet, Haditha, Qa'im and Ramadi)
- the aftermath of the second Fallujah military offensive has been full of promises of compensation and reconstruction. But as yet no significant reconstruction has taken place, although the Anbar Reconstruction Council (established by the Iraqi Government Ministry of Industry) has begun to make strategies for rebuilding the city. Locals have pooled their resources with the support of NGOs and are using donations from other cities to restore minimal standards of daily living.

Mohammed Abdulla of SCHRD paints a dismal picture of the situation in Fallujah: 'The mood is that people will never forget what was done to them and their city. I don't think we'll see the end of this. People will never forget

---

30 Dahr Jamail, *Asia Times*, 3 June 2005.

to have their revenge on the American troops, but they would like to prepare themselves for another attack. This is what the Fallujan negotiators had warned the Americans of. Lack of security, which is ongoing in Iraq now, is one these results.'

Abdulla, like other residents of the city, wondered why the US military would not let unembedded media into Fallujah. 'Why have they not let the media inside Fallujah?,' he asked. 'If America says she is right, then why did she stop two UN investigators from getting inside Fallujah?'[31]

What now seems clear is that the situation in Fallujah has adversely affected other parts of the country, even in formerly quiescent locales such as Basra. The events in this city have in effect jeopardized the reconstruction of a whole nation.

---

31 *Ibid.*

TESTIMONIES

Jo Wilding

The scenes in which Jo appears mirror Jo Wilding's real-life experiences in Iraq.

Jo Wilding is a human rights activist from Bristol, England; she is also a lawyer, writer and clown. In August 2001 Jo went to Iraq to break the sanctions imposed on the country, and it proved to be the first of several visits. Her subsequent diary entries – archived online, at www. wildfirejo.blogspot.com and www.bristolfoe.org.uk/ wildfire – describe in vivid detail the anti-war movement (prior to the attacks in 2003) and, later on, the horrors inflicted upon ordinary Iraqi people by the occupying forces. Despite being obligated to leave Iraq twelve days into the initial bombing by Britain and the US – owing to visa requirements and safety concerns – she returned to the country with a travelling circus. Circus2Iraq proved itself exceptional on three counts: one, by providing humanitarian aid at every opportunity; two, by seeking to inject a small dose of normality into the lives of traumatized Iraqi civilians; and three, by accessing villages and cities otherwise neglected by mainstream news reporters. Now back in the UK, Jo continues to transcribe the stories passed on by her friends working in Iraq.

14 December 2003

www.wildfirejo.blogspot.com/2003_12_01_
wildfirejo_archive.html

The arrest of Saddam

They are saying that Saddam has been caught. The TV stations are showing pictures of an old, grubby, bearded man in captivity. Khalid says it's definitely him. 'He has been on television for twelve hours a day for thirty-five years. I am sure it is him.' Marwan says it's all a trick. 'It's not the real Saddam.'

The woman who begs with her six-year-old daughter flung her arms around me: 'Saddam kelaboutch.' The watch-seller came over to try to give me a kiss as well but I'm not sure that was anything to do with the capture of Saddam. An old woman in a raincoat and a floppy hat stood on the island in the middle of the road twirling a plastic mop. Again, I'm unclear whether that was related to the Saddam issue. Firas was grinning enormously, taking photos of everyone and everything. 'My brother died in Saddam's war with Iran. Now they have caught him.'

There was more than the usual amount of gunfire in the air as word spread, though thankfully less than when the Iraqi football team won a match a while back. The habit of firing into the air at times of celebration scares me more than all the car bombs, thieves and twitchy Americans put together. A man crossing the road crossed his wrists to signify handcuffs and called out 'Saddam kelabach' through the window. Kerim, the driver, asked did I think it was true? 'Saddam kelabach?'

I haven't yet met anyone with any pity for him, though I haven't been yet to the main areas of resistance, but I haven't seen the dancing I thought I'd see in the streets while I've been driving around town this afternoon. The petrol queues are longer than ever and even smiles were a blessed break from the weariness of the struggle for basics. Kerim says eight hours is a good run from the queue's end to the pump. The 960km drive to the Jordanian border can be done in four and a half. Iraqi police shield the US tanks on sentry duty outside empty petrol stations. When fuel arrives, Kerim says, sometimes it only lasts an hour or two and then no one moves until another tanker arrives.

Khalid said they should make Saddam crawl over nails. We passed a portrait with his face painted over and Hamsa said, 'Poor you. Now you are in handcuffs, you bastard.' For me, I want to see his trial. I want to hear him tell the truth. I want to hear the whole truth. I want us to learn from this and never let it happen to people again, that they live under such a man.

11 April 2004

www.wildfirejo.blogspot.com/2004_04_01_
wildfirejo_archive.html

Fallujah
Posted 13 April 2004

US snipers in Fallujah shoot unarmed man in the back, old woman with white flag, children fleeing their homes and the ambulance that we were going in to fetch a woman in premature labour.

Trucks, oil tankers, tanks are burning on the highway east to Fallujah. A stream of boys and men goes to and from a lorry that's not burnt, stripping it bare. We turn onto the back roads through Abu Ghraib, Nuha and Ahrar singing in Arabic, past the vehicles full of people and a few possessions, heading the other way, past the improvised refreshment posts along the way where boys throw food through the windows into the bus for us and for the people still inside Fallujah.

The bus is following a car with the nephew of a local sheikh and a guide who has contacts with the Mujahedin and has cleared this with them. The reason I'm on the bus is that a journalist I knew turned up at my door at about 11 at night telling me things were desperate in Fallujah, he'd been bringing out children with their limbs blown off, the US soldiers were going around telling people to leave by dusk or be killed, but then when people fled with what-ever they could carry, they were being stopped at the US military checkpoint on the edge of town and not let out, trapped, watching the sun go down.

He said aid vehicles and the media were being turned away. He said there was some medical aid that needed to go in and there was a better chance of it getting there with foreigners, Westerners, to get through the American checkpoints. The rest of the way was secured with the armed groups who control the roads we'd travel on. We'd take in the medical supplies, see what else we could do to help and then use the bus to bring out people who needed to leave.

I'll spare you the whole decision-making process, all the questions we all asked ourselves and each other, and you can spare me the accusations of madness, but what it came down to was this: if I don't do it, who will? Either way, we arrive in one piece.

We pile the stuff in the corridor and the boxes are torn open straightaway, the blankets most welcomed. It's not a hospital at all but a clinic, a private doctor's surgery treating people free since air strikes destroyed the town's main hospital. Another has been improvised in a car garage. There's no anaesthetic. The blood bags are in a drinks fridge and the doctors warm them up under the hot tap in an unhygienic toilet.

***

Screaming women come in, praying, slapping their chests and faces. 'Ummi' – my mother – one cries. I hold her until Maki, a consultant and acting director of the clinic, brings me to the bed where a child of about ten is lying with a bullet wound to the head. A smaller child is being treated for a similar injury in the next bed. A US sniper hit them and their grandmother as they left their home to flee Fallujah.

The lights go out, the fan stops and in the sudden quiet someone holds up the flame of a cigarette lighter for the doctor to carry on operating by. The electricity to the town has been cut off for days and when the generator runs out of petrol they just have to manage till it comes back on. Dave quickly donates his torch. The children are not going to live.

'Come,' says Maki and ushers me alone into a room where an old woman has just had an abdominal bullet wound stitched up. Another [wound] in her leg is being dressed, the bed under her foot soaked with blood, a white flag still clutched in her hand and the same story: I was leaving my home to go to Baghdad when I was hit by a US sniper. Some of the town is held by US Marines, other parts by the local fighters. Their homes are in the US controlled area and they are adamant that the snipers were US Marines.

Snipers are causing not just carnage but also the paralysis of the ambulance and evacuation services. The biggest hospital after the main one was bombed is in US territory and cut off from the clinic by snipers. The ambulance has been repaired four times after bullet damage. Bodies are lying in the streets because no one can go to collect them without being shot.

Some said we were mad to come to Iraq; quite a few said we were completely insane to come to Fallujah and now there are people telling me that getting in the back of the pick-up to go past the snipers and get sick and injured people is the craziest thing they've ever seen. I know, though, that if we don't, no one will.

He's holding a white flag with a red crescent on; I don't know his name. The men we pass wave us on when the driver explains where we're going. The silence is ferocious in the no man's land between the pick-up at the edge of the Mujahedin territory, which has just gone from our sight around the last corner and the Marines' line beyond the next wall; no birds, no music, no indication that anyone is still living until a gate opens opposite and a woman comes out, points.

We edge along to the hole in the wall where we can see the car, spent mortar shells around it. The feet are visible, crossed, in the gutter. I think he's dead already. The snipers are visible too, two of them on the corner of the building. As yet I think they can't see us so we need to let them know we're there.

'Hello,' I bellow at the top of my voice. 'Can you hear me?' They must. They're about 30 metres from us, maybe less, and it's so still you could hear the flies buzzing at fifty paces. I repeat myself a few times, still without reply, so decide to explain myself a bit more.

'We are a medical team. We want to remove this wounded man. Is it OK for us to come out and get him? Can you give us a signal that it's OK?'

I'm sure they can hear me but they're still not responding. Maybe they didn't understand it all, so I say the same again. Dave yells too in his US accent. I yell again. Finally I think I hear a shout back. Not sure, I call again.

'Hello.'

'Yeah.'

'Can we come out and get him?'

'Yeah.'

Slowly, our hands up, we go out. The black cloud that rises to greet us carries with it a hot, sour smell. Solidified, his legs are heavy. I leave them to Rana and Dave, our guide lifting under his hips. The Kalashnikov is attached by sticky blood to his hair and hand and we don't want it with us so I put my foot on it as I pick up his shoulders and his blood falls out through the hole in his back. We heave him into the pick-up as best we can and try to outrun the flies.

I suppose he was wearing flip flops because he's barefoot now, no more than twenty years old, in imitation Nike pants [trousers] and a blue and black striped football shirt with a big 28 on the back. As the orderlies from the clinic pull the young fighter off the pick-up, yellow fluid pours from his mouth and they flip him over, face up, the way into the clinic clearing in front of them, straight up the ramp into the makeshift morgue.

We wash the blood off our hands and get in the ambulance. There are people trapped in the other hospital who need to go to Baghdad. Siren screaming, lights flashing, we huddle on the floor of the ambulance, passports and ID cards held out the windows. We pack it with people, one with his chest taped together and a drip, one on a stretcher, legs jerking violently so I have to hold them down as we wheel him out, lifting him over steps.

The hospital is better able to treat them than the clinic but hasn't got enough of anything to sort them out properly and the only way to get them to Baghdad [is] on our bus, which means they have to go to the clinic. We're crammed on the floor of the ambulance in case it's shot at. Nisareen, a woman doctor about my age, can't stop a few tears once we're out.

The doctor rushes out to meet me: 'Can you go to fetch a lady, she is pregnant and she is delivering the baby too soon?'

Azzam is driving, Ahmed in the middle directing him and me by the window, the visible foreigner, the passport. Something scatters across my hand, simultaneous with the crashing of a bullet through the ambulance, some plastic part dislodged, flying through the window.

We stop, turn off the siren, keep the blue light flashing, wait, eyes on the silhouettes of men in US Marine uniforms on the corners of the buildings. Several shots come. We duck, get as low as possible and I can see tiny red lights whipping past the window, past my head. Some, it's hard to tell, are hitting the ambulance. I start singing. What else do you do when someone's shooting at you? A tyre bursts with an enormous noise and a jerk of the vehicle.

I'm outraged. We're trying to get to a woman who's giving birth without any medical attention, without electricity, in a city under siege, in a clearly marked ambulance, and you're shooting at us. How dare you? How dare you?

Azzam grabs the gear stick and gets the ambulance into reverse, another tyre bursting as we go over the ridge in the centre of the road, the shots still coming as we flee around the corner. I carry on singing. The wheels are scraping, burst rubber burning on the road.

The men run for a stretcher as we arrive and I shake my head. They spot the new bullet holes and run to see if we're OK. Is there any other way to get to her, I want to know. 'La, maaku tarieq.' There is no other way. They say we did the right thing. They say they've fixed the ambulance four times already and they'll fix it again but the radiator's gone and the wheels are buckled and she's still at home in the dark giving birth alone. I let her down.

We can't go out again. For one thing there's no ambulance and besides it's dark now and that means our foreign faces can't protect the people who go out with us or the people we pick up. Maki is the acting director of the place. He says he hated Saddam but now he hates the Americans more.

We take off the blue gowns as the sky starts exploding somewhere beyond the building opposite. Minutes later a car roars up to the clinic. I can hear him screaming before I can see that there's no skin left on his body. He's burnt from head to foot. For sure there's nothing they can do. He'll die of dehydration within a few days.

Another man is pulled from the car onto a stretcher. Cluster bombs, they say, although it's not clear whether they mean one or both of them. We set off walking to Mr Yasser's house, waiting at each corner for someone to check the street before we cross. A ball of fire falls from a plane, splits into smaller balls of bright white lights. I think they're cluster bombs, because cluster bombs are in the front of my mind, but they vanish, just magnesium flares, incredibly bright but short-lived, giving a flash picture of the town from above.

Yasser asks us all to introduce ourselves. I tell him I'm training to be a lawyer. One of the other men asks whether I know about international law. They want to know about the law on war crimes, what a war crime is. I tell them I know some of the Geneva Conventions, that I'll bring some information next time I come and we can get someone to explain it in Arabic.

We bring up the matter of Nayoko. This group of fighters has nothing to do with the ones who are holding the Japanese hostages, but while they're thanking us for what we did this evening, we talk about the things Nayoko did for the street kids, how much they loved her. They can't promise anything but that they'll try and find out where she is and try to persuade the group to let her and the others go. I don't suppose it will make any difference. They're busy fighting a war in Fallujah. They're unconnected with the other group. But it can't hurt to try.

The planes are above us all night so that as I doze I forget I'm not on a long distance flight, the constant bass note of an unmanned reconnaissance drone overlaid with the frantic thrash of jets and the dull beat of helicopters and interrupted by the explosions.

In the morning I make balloon dogs, giraffes and elephants for the little one, Abdullah Aboudi, who's clearly distressed by the noise of the aircraft and explosions. I blow bubbles which he follows with his eyes. Finally, finally, I score a smile. The twins, thirteen years old, laugh too, one of them an ambulance driver, both said to be handy with a Kalashnikov.

The doctors look haggard in the morning. None has slept more than a couple of hours a night for a week. One has had only eight hours of sleep in the last seven days, missing the funerals of his brother and aunt because he was needed at the hospital.

'The dead we cannot help,' Jassim said. 'I must worry about the injured.'

We go again, Dave, Rana, and me, this time in a pick-up. There are some sick people close to the Marines' line who need evacuating. No one dares come out of their house because the Marines are on top of the buildings shooting at anything that moves. Saad fetches us a white flag and tells us not to worry, he's checked and secured the road, no Mujahedin will fire at us, that peace is upon us, this eleven-year-old child, his face covered with a keffiyeh, but for his bright brown eyes, his AK-47 almost as tall as he is.

We shout again to the soldiers, hold up the flag with a red crescent sprayed onto it. Two come down from the building, cover this side and Rana mutters, 'Allahu akbar. Please nobody take a shot at them.'

We jump down and tell them we need to get some sick people from the houses and they want Rana to go and bring out the family from the house whose roof they're on. Thirteen women and children are still inside, in one room, without food and water for the last twenty-four hours.

'We're going to be going through soon clearing the houses,' the senior one says.

'What does that mean, clearing the houses?'

'Going into every one searching for weapons.' He's checking his watch, can't tell me what will start when, of course, but there's going to be air strikes in support. 'If you're going to do this you gotta do it soon.'

First we go down the street we were sent to. There's a man, face down, in a white dishdasha, a small round red stain on his back. We run to him. Again the flies have got there first. Dave is at his shoulders, I'm by his knees and as we reach to roll him onto the stretcher Dave's hand goes through his chest, through the cavity left by the bullet that entered so neatly through his back and blew his heart out.

There's no weapon in his hand. Only when we arrive, his sons come out, crying, shouting. He was unarmed, they scream. He was unarmed. He just went out the gate and they shot him. None of them have dared come out since. No one had dared come to get his body, horrified, terrified, forced to violate the traditions of treating the body immediately. They couldn't have known we were coming so it's inconceivable that anyone came out and retrieved a weapon but left the body. He was unarmed, fifty-five years old, shot in the back.

We cover his face, carry him to the pick-up. There's nothing to cover his body with. The sick woman is helped out of the house, the little girls around her hugging cloth bags to their bodies, whispering, 'Baba. Baba.' Daddy. Shaking, they let us go first, hands up, around the corner, then we usher them to the cab of the pick-up, shielding their heads so they can't see him, the cuddly fat man stiff in the back.

The people seem to pour out of the houses now in the hope we can escort them safely out of the line of fire, kids, women, men, anxiously asking us whether they can all go, or only the women and children. We go to ask. The young Marine tells us that men of fighting age can't leave. What's fighting age, I want to know. He contemplates. Anything under forty-five. No lower limit.

It appals me that all those men would be trapped in a city which is about to be destroyed. Not all of them are fighters, not all are armed. It's going to happen out of the view of the world, out of sight of the media, because most of the media in Fallujah is embedded with the Marines or turned away at the outskirts. Before we can pass the message on, two explosions scatter the crowd in the side street back into their houses.

Rana's with the Marines evacuating the family from the house they're occupying. The pick-up isn't back yet. The families are hiding behind their walls. We wait, because there's nothing else we can do. We wait in no man's land. The Marines, at least, are watching us through binoculars; maybe the local fighters are too.

I've got a disappearing hanky in my pocket so while I'm sitting like a lemon, nowhere to go, gunfire and explosions aplenty all around, I make the hanky disappear, reappear, disappear. It's always best, I think, to seem completely unthreatening and completely unconcerned, so no one worries about you enough to shoot. We can't wait too long though. Rana's been gone ages. We have to go and get her to hurry. There's a young man in the group. She's talked them into letting him leave too.

A man wants to use his police car to carry some of the people, a couple of elderly ones who can't walk far, the smallest children. It's missing a door. Who knows if it was really a police car or the car was reappropriated and just ended up there? It didn't matter if it got more people out faster. They creep from their houses, huddle by the wall, follow us out, their hands up too, and walk up the street clutching babies, bags, each other.

The pick-up gets back and we shovel as many onto it as we can as an ambulance arrives from somewhere. A young man waves from the doorway of what's left of a house, his upper body bare, a blood- soaked bandage around his arm, probably a fighter but it makes no difference once someone is wounded and unarmed. Getting the dead isn't essential. Like the doctor said, the dead don't need help, but if it's easy enough then we will. Since we're already OK with the soldiers and the ambulance is here, we run down to fetch them in. It's important in Islam to bury the body straightaway.

The ambulance follows us down. The soldiers start shouting in English at us for it to stop, pointing guns. It's moving fast. We're all yelling, signalling for it to stop but it seems to take forever for the driver to hear and see us. It stops. It stops, before they open fire. We haul them onto the stretchers and run, shove them in the back. Rana squeezes in the front with the wounded man and Dave and I crouch in the back beside the bodies. He says he had allergies as a kid and hasn't got much sense of smell. I wish, retrospectively, for childhood allergies, and stick my head out the window.

The bus is going to leave, taking the injured people back to Baghdad, the man with the burns, one of the women who was shot in the jaw and shoulder by a sniper, several others. Rana says she's staying to help. Dave and I don't hesitate: we're staying too. 'If I don't do it, who will?' has become an accidental motto and I'm acutely aware after the last foray how many people, how many women and children, are still in their houses either because they've got nowhere to go, because they're scared to go out of the door or because they've chosen to stay.

To begin with it's agreed, then Azzam says we have to go. He hasn't got contacts with every armed group, only with some. There are different issues to square with each one. We need to get these people back to Baghdad as quickly as we can. If we're kidnapped or killed it will cause even more problems, so it's better that we just get on the bus and leave and come back with him as soon as possible.

It hurts to climb onto the bus when the doctor has just asked us to go and evacuate some more people. I hate the fact that a qualified medic can't travel in the ambulance but I can, just because I look like the sniper's sister or one of his mates, but that's the way it is today and the way it was yesterday and I feel like a traitor for leaving, but I can't see where I've got a choice. It's a war now and as alien as it is to me to do what I'm told, for once I've got to.

Jassim is scared. He harangues Mohammed constantly, tries to pull him out of the driver's seat while we're moving. The woman with the gunshot wound is on the back seat, the man with the burns in front of her, being fanned with cardboard from the empty boxes, his intravenous drips swinging from the rail along the ceiling of the bus. It's hot. It must be unbearable for him. Saad comes onto the bus to wish us well for the journey. He shakes Dave's hand and then mine. I hold his in both of mine and tell him 'Dir balak,' take care, as if I could say anything more stupid to a pre-teen Mujahedin with an AK-47 in his other hand, and our eyes meet and stay fixed, his full of fire and fear.

Can't I take him away? Can't I take him somewhere he can be a child? Can't I make him a balloon giraffe and give him some drawing pens and tell him not to forget to brush his teeth? Can't I find the person who put the rifle in the hands of that little boy? Can't I tell someone about what that does to a child? Do I have to leave him here where there are heavily armed men all around him and lots of them are not on his side, however many sides there are in all of this? And of course I do. I do have to leave him, like child soldiers everywhere.

The way back is tense, the bus almost getting stuck in a dip in the sand, people escaping in anything, even piled on the trailer of a tractor, lines of cars and pick-ups and buses ferrying people to the dubious sanctuary of Baghdad, lines of men in vehicles queuing to get back into the city having got their families to safety, either to fight or to help evacuate more people. The driver, Jassim, the father, ignores Azzam and takes a different road so that suddenly we're not following the lead car and we're on a road that's controlled by a different armed group than the ones which know us.

A crowd of men waves guns to stop the bus. Somehow they apparently believe that there are American soldiers on the bus, as if they wouldn't be in tanks or helicopters, and there are men getting out of their cars with shouts of 'Sahafa Amreeki,' American journalists. The passengers shout out of the windows, 'Ana min Fallujah,' I am from Fallujah. Gunmen run onto the bus and see that it's true, there are sick and injured and old people, Iraqis, and then relax, wave us on.

We stop in Abu Ghraib and swap seats, foreigners in the front, Iraqis less visible, headscarves off so we look more Western. The American soldiers are so happy to see Westerners they don't mind too much about the Iraqis with us, search the men and the bus, leave the women unsearched because there are no women soldiers to search us. Mohammed keeps asking me if things are going to be OK. 'Al-melaach wiyana,' I tell him. The angels are with us. He laughs.

And then we're in Baghdad, delivering them to the hospitals, Nuha in tears as they take the burnt man off groaning and whimpering. She puts her arms around me and asks me to be her friend. I make her feel less isolated, she says, less alone. And the satellite news says the cease-fire is holding and George Bush says to the troops on Easter Sunday that, 'I know what we're doing in Iraq is right.' Shooting unarmed men in the back outside their family home is right? Shooting grandmothers with white flags is right? Shooting at women and children who are fleeing their homes is right? Firing at ambulances is right?

Well George, I know too now. I know what it looks like when you brutalize people so much that they've nothing left to lose. I know what it looks like when an operation is being done without anaesthetic because the hospitals are destroyed or under sniper fire and the city's under siege and aid isn't getting in properly. I know what it sounds like too. I know what it looks like when tracer bullets are passing your head, even though you're in an ambulance. I know what it looks like when a man's chest is no longer inside him and what it smells like and I know what it looks like when his wife and children pour out of his house. It's a crime and it's a disgrace to us all.

17 April 2004

www.wildfirejo.blogspot.com/2004_04_01_wildfirejo_
archive.html

Posted 20 April 2004

Sergeant Tratner of the First Armoured Division is irri-tated. 'Git back or you'll git killed,' are his opening words. Lee says we're press and he looks with disdain at the car. 'In this piece of shit?' Makes us less of a target for kidnap-pers, Lee tells him. Suddenly he decides he recognizes Lee from the TV. Based in Germany, he watches the BBC. He sees Lee on TV all the time. 'Cool. Hey, can I have your autograph?'

Lee makes a scribble, unsure who he's meant to be but happy to have a ticket through the checkpoint which all the cars before us have been turned back from, and Sergeant Tratner carries on. 'You guys be careful in Fallujah. We're killing loads of those folks.' Detecting a lack of admiration on our part, he adds, 'Well, they're killing us too. I like Fallujah. I killed a bunch of them motherfuckers.'

I wish Sergeant Tratner were a caricature, a stereotype, but these are all direct quotations. We fiddle with our hijabs in the roasting heat. 'You don't have to wear those things any more,' he says. 'You're liberated now.' He laughs. I mention that more and more women are wearing hijabs nowadays because of increasing attacks on them.

A convoy of aid vehicles flying Red Crescent flags approaches the checkpoint, hesitates. 'We don't like to encourage them,' Sergeant Tratner explains, his tongue loosened by the excitement of finding someone to talk to.

'Jeez it's good to meet someone that speaks English. Well, apart from "Mister" and "please" and "why".'

'Haven't you got translators?' someone asks him.

Sergeant Tratner points his rifle in the direction of the lead vehicle in the convoy. 'I got the best translator in the world,' he says. One ambulance comes through with us, the rest turn back. There are loads of supplies when we get to Fallujah – food, water, medicine – at the clinic and the mosque which have come in on the back roads. The relief effort for the people there has been enormous, but the hospital is in the US-held part of town, cut off from the clinic by sniper fire. They can't get any of the relief supplies in to the hospital nor the injured people out. We load the ambulance with disinfectant, needles, bandages, food and water and set off, equipped this time with loudspeakers, pull up to a street corner and get out. The hospital is to the right, quite a way off; the Marines are to the left. Four of us in blue paper smocks walk out, hands up, calling out that we're a relief team, trying to deliver supplies to the hospital.

There's no response and we walk slowly towards the hospital. We need the ambulance with us because there's more stuff than we can carry, so we call out that we're going to bring an ambulance with us, that we'll walk and the ambulance will follow. The nose of the ambulance edges out into the street, shiny and new, brought in to replace the ones destroyed by sniper fire.

Shots rip down the street, two bangs and a zipping noise uncomfortably close. The ambulance springs back into the side road like it's on a piece of elastic and we dart into the yard of the corner house, out through the side gate so we're back beside the vehicle.

This time we walk away from the hospital towards the Marines, just us and the loudspeaker, no ambulance, to try and talk to them properly. Slowly, slowly, we take steps, shouting that we're unarmed, that we're a relief team, that we're trying to get supplies to the hospital.

Another two shots dissuade us. I'm furious. From behind the wall I inform them that their actions are in breach of the Geneva Conventions. 'How would you feel if it was your sister in that hospital unable to get treated because some man with a gun wouldn't let the medical supplies through.' David takes me away as I'm about to call down a plague of warts on their trigger fingers.

Because it's the most urgent thing to do, we waste the rest of the precious daylight trying to find someone in authority that we can sort it out with. As darkness starts I'm still fuming and the hospital is still without disinfectant. We go into the house behind the clinic and the smell of death chokes me: the dried blood and the putrefying flesh evoking the memory of a few days earlier, sitting in the back of an ambulance with the rotting bodies and the flies.

The aerial bombardment starts with the night and we stand outside watching the explosions and the flames. No one can quite recall whether it's a theoretical cease-fire or not. Someone brings the remains of a rocket, unravelled into metal and wires, a fuel canister inside it, and it sits like a space alien on display on a piece of cloth on the pavement near the clinic while everyone gives it stares and a wide berth.

Someone comes round to give us a report: the Mujahedin have shot down a helicopter and killed fifteen enemy soldiers. During the evening's street fighting twelve American soldiers have been killed. Six hundred were killed in an attack on their base but he can't tell us how, where or when. He says thousands of US soldiers' bodies have been dumped in the desert near Rutba, further east. I don't doubt that the US is under reporting its casualties whenever it thinks it can get away with it but I suspect some over reporting this time. Someone whispers that he's the cousin of 'Comical Ali', the old Minister of Information. It's not true but it ought to be.

The cacophony of planes and explosions goes on through the night. I wake from my doze certain that rockets are being fired from the garden outside our room. Rhythmic, deep, resonating, the barrage goes on and the fear spreads in my belly anticipating an explosion from the air to stop the rockete[e]r. I can't keep still and wait for it so I go outside and realize he's at least a couple of streets away. The noise quietens as if soothed by a song of prayer from the mosque. Someone says that it's a plea to stop shooting. I don't know if it's true, but every time I hear different songs from the minaret I wonder what it means, whether it's a call to prayer, a call to arms, something else, maybe just someone singing the town back to sleep.

In the morning the cease-fire negotiations begin again, centred, like everything else, in one of the local mosques. For eight days, people say, the US army has fought for control of a town of 350,000 people and now, with the fighters still armed in the street, they're trying to negotiate the terms of a cease-fire. A body arrives at the hospital, a wound to the leg and his throat sliced open. The men say he was lying injured in the street and the Marines came and slit his throat. A pick-up races up and a man is pulled out with most of his arm missing, a stump with bits sticking out, pouring blood. He bleeds to death.

Two French journalists have been admitted to the town, under the protection of the mosque, and for their benefit the body is swaddled head to foot in bandages, carried to a van with no back doors and driven away by two boys including Aodeh, one of the twin boys we met on the first trip. Earlier a little girl was brought out, a polka-dotted black headscarf around her face, pink T-shirt under a black sleeveless cardigan with jeans, sparkly bobbles on her gloves, holding a Kalashnikov.

She was clean, her clothes were fresh and she was very cute, eleven years old, and after the photo one of the men, her father I think, took her away as if her job was done. I hope and believe she was only being used as a poster child, that she wasn't really involved in the fighting. She's no younger than the lad from the other day who I know is involved in the fighting, but I wish he wasn't either.

While we wait we chat with the sheikh in the mosque. He says the hospitals have recorded 1,200 casualties, between 5-600 people dead in the first five days of fighting and eighty-six children killed in the first three days of fighting. There's no knowing how many have been hurt or killed in areas held by the US. A heavily pregnant woman was killed by a missile, her unborn child saved, the sheikh says, but already orphaned.

'Fallujah people like peace but after we were attacked by the US they lost all their friends here. We had a few trained officers and soldiers from the old army, but now everyone has joined the effort. Not all of the men are fighting: some left with their families, some work in the clinics or move supplies or go in the negotiating teams. We are willing to fight until the last minute, even if it takes a hundred years.'

He says the official figure is 25% of the town controlled by the Marines: 'This is made up of small parts, a bit
in the north east, a bit in the south east, the part around
the entrance to the town, controlled with snipers and light
vehicles.' The new unity between Shia and Sunni pleases
him: 'Fallujah is Iraq and Iraq is Fallujah. We received a
delegation from all the governorates of Iraq to give aid and
solidarity.'

The cease-fire takes effect from 9am. Those with vehicles
are loading stuff from the storage building opposite the
mosque and moving it around the town. The opening up
of the way to the hospital is one of the terms of the deal,
so we're not really needed anymore. As well it's starting to
feel like there are different agendas being pursued that we
could all too easily get caught up in, other people's politics
and power struggles, so we decide to leave.

At the corner of town is a fork, a paved road curving
round in front of the last of the houses, a track leading into
the desert, the latter controlled by the Marines, who fire a
warning shot when our driver gets out to negotiate a way
through; the former by as yet invisible Mujahedin. The
crossfire suddenly surrounds the car. David, head down,
shifts into the driver's seat and backs us out of there but
the only place to go is into the line of Mujahedin. One of
the fighters jumps into the passenger seat and directs us.

'We're hostages, aren't we?' Billie says.

No, it's fine, I say, sure that they're just directing us out
of harm's way. The man in the passenger seat asks which
country we're all from. Donna says she's Australian. Billie
says she's British.

'Allahu akbar! Ahlan wa sahlan.' Translated, it's
more or less, God is great. I'm pleased to meet you.

The others don't know the words but the drift is clear enough: 'I think he just said he's got the two most valuable hostages in the world,' Billie paraphrases. We get out of the car, which in any case feels a bit uncomfortable now there's a man with a keffiyeh round his head pointing a loaded rocket launcher at it. They bring a jeep and as I climb in I can't help noticing that the driver has a grenade between his legs. I'm sure it's intended for the Americans, not for us, but nonetheless it's clear there's no room for dissent.

Still, it's not till we turn off the road back to the mosque and stop at a house, not until David and the other men are being searched, not really until a couple of the fighters take off their keffiyehs to tie the men's hands behind their backs, that I accept that I'm definitely a captive.

What do you do when you're kidnapped in Iraq? What do you do? You look for ways out. You wonder whether they're going to kill you, make demands for your release, if they'll hurt you. You wait for the knives and the guns and the video camera. You tell yourself you're going to be OK. You think about your family, your mum finding out you're kidnapped. You decide you're going to be strong, because there's nothing else you can do. You fight the understanding that your life isn't fully in your hands any more, that you can't control what's happening. You turn to your best friend next to you and tell her you love her, with all your heart.

And then I'm put in a different car from her and I can only hope they take us to the same place and try in vain to notice where we're going, recognize some landmarks, but the truth is that I'm without any sense of direction at all and have trouble remembering left from right, even on a good day, but in any case there's no one on the streets but fighters, nowhere to hide.

Donna, Billie, David, Ahrar and I are delivered to another house, cushions around the walls of a big room, a bed at one end of the room beside a cabinet of crockery and ornaments. A tall, dignified man in a brown keffiyeh sits and begins interviewing Donna, her name, where she's from, what she does there, what she's doing in Iraq, why she came to Fallujah.

He decides to separate us, has the others move me, David and Billie into the next room under the guard of a man in jeans too loose for his skinny body, trainers and a shirt, his face covered except for his eyes. It's not much to go on but I doubt he's beyond late teens, a little nervous, calmed by our calmness. After a while he decides he shouldn't let us talk to each other, signals for silence. Billie's not well, hot and sick. She lies down on the cushions, head on her arm. The fighter brings a pillow and gently lifts her head onto it, takes all the stuff off the cushions so he can fold the blanket over her. The other one brings a cotton sheet and unfolds the blanket, covers her with the sheet and then replaces the blanket around her: tucked in by the Mujahedin.

It's my turn next for questioning. I feel OK. All I can tell him is the truth. He wants to know the same things: where I live, what I'm doing in Iraq, what I'm doing in Fallujah, so I tell him about the circus, about the ambulance trips, about the snipers shooting at us. Then he asks what the British people think about the war. I'm not sure what the right answer is. I don't know what the national opinion is these days. I try to compute what's least likely to make him think it's worth keeping me.

If people oppose the occupation, he says, how is it that the government could carry on and do it. He's genuinely interested but also sarcastic: surely the great liberators must be truly democratic, truly governing by the will of the people? Instead of the extended version of Jo's rant about the UK constitution he starts asking about Billie. I know what her answers will be so it's easy. I dodge the issue when he moves on to David and hope he won't press me. I don't know him very well, I say, because I don't know if he wants to mention that he's also a journalist. I tell the man I've just met him. I just know him as Martinez.

He thanks me and we're done. David's next. Donna, Billie and I talk quietly about the interviews and the boy guarding us doesn't object. Someone asks if we want chai. Warm giggles come from the kitchen; maybe the two young men imagining that their mates could see them now, masked, Kalashnikov-wielding, brewing tea for a load of women.

David's interview is short and when I come back from the outside toilet, still alert for an escape route, as improbable as I know it is, the others are all back in the main room again and the tea is ready. Billie's bag comes in to be fished through, a camera, a minidisc recorder. The man goes through the pictures on the camera, the missile outside the clinic and a few from Baghdad, listens to the interview with the sheikh on the minidisc.

Donna's camera has similar pictures of the missile, some of the street kids, some from around the flat. The tape in the video camera is from the opening of the new youth centre in al-Daura, backing up her testimony that she's the director of an organization which sets up projects for kids. The other tape contains a performance by the Boom-chucka Circus, backing up mine that I'm a clown.

No one brings in my bag or David's. I think it's best not to mention this, in case there's anything to offend them in either of them. In particular I think it's best they don't notice anyone's passport in case it encourages them to look for all our passports because Billie's contains a stamp from Israel. It's from when she was working in Palestine but it's better not to spark the suspicion in the first place.

Ahrar, the questioning over, is close to hysterical. She's more frightened of her family's reaction to her having been out all the previous night than of the armed men holding us. We cuddle and stroke and pacify her as best we can, tell her we'll tell her family it wasn't her fault. The trouble was that, by the time we left Baghdad to come here, it was already too late for her to get home the same evening, and now she's afraid it's going to be a second night.

I quietly start singing, unsure whether that's allowed. The others join in where they know the words. By the end of the song her sobs have stopped and her only word is, 'Continue,' so we do, song after song until the prayer call begins and it's impolite to sing at the same time.

Ahrar gets tearful again. Donna tries to comfort her. 'I have a big faith in God,' she says.

'Yes, but you don't know Mama,' Ahrar wails.

Before the war and before we came to Fallujah the first time I remember feeling that it's impossible to know how you'll react to something like being under fire. I couldn't have imagined either how I'd react to this, this unpredictable situation, these masked and armed men, the fear, the uncertainty. Repeatedly they tell us not to be afraid, 'We are Moslems. We will not hurt you.'

Still my instinct tells me I'm going to be OK. Still my mind wanders to the question of whether they'll shoot us against a wall or just open fire in the room, whether they'll take us out one by one or we'll all be killed together, whether they'll save the bullets and cut our throats, how long it hurts for when you're shot, if it's instantly over or if there's some echo of the agony of the metal ripping through your flesh after your life is gone.

I don't need those thoughts and I push them out of my way because I know the others are going through the same thoughts: what's this going to do to my mum? What's going to happen? What's it going to feel like? It wouldn't be fair to mention it aloud so there's nothing to do but sit and stew with it and there's nothing we can do about this situation but wait it out and keep our heads together.

But what I tell myself is this: I can't change the course of this at the moment and if they do point a rifle at me or hold a knife to my throat and I know it's the last moment of my life then for sure there's nothing I can do then I'm determined not to beg or flinch because I was right to come to Fallujah and to try to evacuate people and get supplies to the hospitals and to die for trying to do that isn't ideal but it's OK.

They bring our bags in and I make a hanky disappear. The guard, a different one now, is unimpressed. It's black magic. It's haram [sinful]. It's an affront to Allah. Oops. I show him the secret of the trick in the hope he'll let me off. Instead I make a balloon giraffe for his kids, who he's taken away to the safety of Baghdad.

'My brother was killed and my brother's son and my sister's son. My other brother is in the prison at Abu Ghraib. I am the last one left. Can you imagine? And this

morning my best friend was killed. He was wounded in the
leg and lying in the street and the Americans came and cut
his throat.' That was the one who came into the hospital
this morning. Oh shit. Why wouldn't they kill us?

But the day goes by and we carry on breathing, dozing,
talking. They bring food, apologize for not bringing more,
promise again that they're not going to hurt us. As it gets
dark, behind the windows partly blocked by sandbags,
they light a paraffin lamp. The room gets hotter and hotter
and it's a relief when they take us out to the car to move
again, although change feels somehow threatening at the
same time.

The new house is huge, with electricity. The four women
are shown to a room and David has to stay in the main
room with the men. This was his biggest fear all along,
being separated from the rest of us. We take off the hijabs
that we've kept on all day. One of the men knocks on the
door and, looking at the ground, tells us they've checked
everything and, InshaaAllah, we'll be taken back to
Baghdad in the morning. They can't let us go now because
we'll be kidnapped by some other group.

They feed us, bring us tea, supply us with blankets and
we find pretexts and excuses to nip through the main room
to check on David, bringing him half an orange, a chunk
of chocolate, so he knows we're still thinking of him. He's
more vulnerable than us because we've got each other to
laugh and sing and talk with. Everything that's happened,
although you can never be sure, says they're not going to
hurt women. David's not so comfortable.

The night is filled with the racket of what sounds like
a huge dodgy plumbing system somewhere beyond the
house, a rhythmic series of explosions in quick succession

like an immense grinding noise: apparently it's the sound
of cluster bombs. Billie and I hold each other's hands all
night because we can. In the morning there's still a knot of
doubt in my belly. They said they'd take us home after the
morning prayers, more or less at first light, and it's been
light for ages. Maybe they just told us we'd be released to
keep us calm and quiet.

But they do let us go: they take us to one of the local
imams who says he will drive us home. At the edge of
Fallujah is a queue of vehicles, some already turning back
from the checkpoint. The passengers say the US soldiers
fired as they approached. We get out of the car, hijabs off,
and start the whole rigmarole again, loudspeaker, hands
up, through the maze of concrete and wire, shouting that
we're an international group of ambulance volunteers
trying to leave Fallujah, we're unarmed and please don't
shoot us.

Eventually we can see the soldiers; eventually they lower
the guns, tell us to put our hands down, they're not going
to shoot us. 'My bad,' one says. Apparently it's US slang
for acknowledging your own mistake. 'We're not going to
fire any more warning shots.' We tell them we've got two
cars to bring through and ask about the rest of the cars.
They agree to open up the checkpoint to women, children
and old men. The trouble is, most of the women don't
drive and so can't leave unless their husbands are allowed
to drive them. We persuade them to let through cars with
a male driver even if he is 'of fighting age' if he's got his
family with him.

The fear in Fallujah is that, when most of the women
and children are gone, the town is going to be destroyed
and everyone killed, by massive aerial bombardment or

with a thermobaric weapon or something. Ahrar tries to explain that the men who want to leave are the ones who don't want to fight.

'Oh, we want to keep them in there,' the Marine says. 'There's fighters coming from all over Iraq into Fallujah and we want to keep them all in there so we can kill them all more easily.'

But these are the ones who want to get out, those of the locals who don't want to fight. It doesn't matter though: we've got all we're going to get out of them. We tell the crowd of anxious refugees and leave another local imam as the go-between. The road is quiet but for our small convoy until another roadblock. The imam talks to some locals, tells Ahrar there are Americans ahead. Hijabs off again, we heave ourselves out of the car for another round.

In the sickly, hot silence there are a few cracks but no responses to our shouts. Dust erupts from a house a way off and we wonder if we're walking into a battle. Shouting in English, trying to be as obviously foreign as possible is the only tactic for walking into Marines' lines but it's a bit of a risk when the lines are not clear. We keep yelling for them to give us a wave if they can hear us. There's no response.

'Wait a minute,' David says. 'Are those Marines or are they Muja?'

Oh shit. Tell us we're not walking into a Mujahedin line. We hesitate. Maybe we need to go back to the car and get the imam to come instead.

'No, I think it's OK. I think they're Marines.'

'Decide! Tell us!' As if he's got any more information than the rest of us.

The men we can see start gesturing, big arm movements, pointing to their left, our right, go towards the bridge. It's a signal, which we've been asking for, but it doesn't mean they're not another group of kidnappers. Finally one yells. They're Green Berets, which is why they didn't quite look like the Marines we'd got used to. Billie and I go back towards the cars to signal for them to come. No one fancies walking the aching gap between us and them again, but for time and time and time the cars don't move, despite our arm waving, my roaring through the megaphone. Finally they shift and we scurry back into the relative cover of the bushes around the bridge. 'Are you crazy?' asks one of the soldiers.

I feel a bit closer to insanity than I did before that walk into the unknown, I have to confess, as mortars thunder out of their encampment. He tells me not to worry, they're outgoing. Of course there's some comfort in this. An outgoing mortar is preferable in many ways to an incoming one, but it seems at the same time like a bit of an invitation, RSVP written all over it.

Past them, the second car leaves us. David hugs the driver like he'd just brought him back from the dead and joins us in our car. There's still Abu Ghraib, still Shuala, still who knows what between us and home. Ahrar wants to stop and phone her mum from a roadside booth in the middle of Shuala and even the imam is looking panicky as the call drags on, his carload of foreigners just sitting waiting for someone to notice us. Exhausted and exhibiting the early symptoms of tetchiness, we drag her back to the car and escape.

It's only when we walk through the door of our apartment that we're sure we're coming home, all of us yelling and talking at once, telling the story, laughing over the surreal moments, hugging each other, retrieving hidden passports from underwear.

'We're laughing about it now,' Billie says, 'but there were moments...'

On the news they say Nayoko and the other Japanese hostages have been released, that Watanabi, the Japanese photographer who hung out with us when we took the circus to Samawa, has disappeared with a colleague. They say the cease-fire is holding in Fallujah. Harb comes round to tell me off, but I'm unrepentant. I still think it was the right thing to do.

They took us because we were foreigners acting strangely in the middle of their war. They found out what we were doing and let us go. On the way out we were able to open up the checkpoint which meant people were able to get out of Fallujah to safety. If that was all we did it would still have been worth it. But still in a quiet moment later on I whisper a thank you to the cheeky angels who look after clowns and ambulance volunteers.

8 May 2004

http://electroniciraq.net/news/1490.shtml

Bombs and Goodbyes

I've moved down the street. This has mainly advantages but one notable disadvantage in that I'm a couple of hundred metres closer to 'The Green Zone', as in 'They're bombing the...' The Green Zone, for those who have never needed to know, is the heavily fortified bit which most of the decision-makers and foreign workers in the Coalition Provisional Authority (CPA) never leave because of a theory that it's somehow more dangerous to be on the streets of Baghdad than walled into the most heavily attacked part of it.

Sure enough, first thing in the morning there was a car bomb just outside it. Another advantage of the new apartment is that there's a generator right outside my window, powering a roaring air conditioner. The Fourteenth of July Bridge provides access from Abu Nawas Street, across the Tigris, and soldiers manning the checkpoint approach the cars waiting to cross. It seems the soldier came as usual to look in the car before it reached the checkpoint and the driver detonated it, killing himself, the soldier and six other Iraqis.

In Fallujah they are still finding bodies, bodies in the rubble of the houses crushed by aerial bombing by the US in al-Julan, Hay Askeri and Shuhada, bodies buried in gardens, bodies being brought to the football fields turned into cemeteries. There are some very tiny graves. There are people still missing. The 600-deaths estimate put out by most of the media seems on the low side.

If the killings of four US mercenaries were the reason for the attack on Fallujah then the ratio is at least 150 Iraqis to one American, maybe 250. From the other side, the Iraqi side, the resistance side, the Iraqi life is worth more. If the killings of eighteen Fallujans shortly before the killings of the mercenaries were the spark for the latter then one American life is worth just four-and-a-half Iraqis, a little less than the six-to-one of the car bombing.

There is, of course, a difference between armed self-defence when your town is being invaded, like Fallujah, and setting off bombs in the street but in the end it comes down to this: there has been enough killing. There has been too much killing.

December 2004

www.wildfirejo.blogspot.com/2004_12_01_wildfirejo_
archive.html

This is a reply from Naomi Klein to the US acting ambassador who wrote to the UK *Guardian* newspaper in response to one of Naomi's columns, in which she accused the US of eliminating witnesses in Fallujah. I'm forwarding it because it's important and also accords with what we saw in Fallujah in April. Two unembedded French journalists we met – the only unembedded foreign journalists who were there – were taken prisoner by the US troops and held, blindfolded and filmed with their own camera equipment to prevent them continuing to record what was happening in Fallujah.

...

When asked about Al-Jazeera and Al-Arabiya's reports that hundreds of civilians had been killed in Fallujah, Donald Rumsfeld, the US secretary of defence, replied that 'what Al-Jazeera is doing is vicious, inaccurate and inexcusable ... ' Last month, US troops once again laid siege to Fallujah – but this time the attack included a new tactic: eliminating the doctors, journalists and clerics who focused public attention on civilian casualties last time around.

...

Eliminating Journalists
The images from last month's siege on Fallujah came almost exclusively from reporters embedded with US troops. This is because Arab journalists who had covered April's siege from the civilian perspective had effectively been

eliminated. Al-Jazeera had no cameras on the ground because it has been banned from reporting in Iraq indefinitely. Al-Arabiya did have an unembedded reporter, Abdel Kader al-Saadi, in Fallujah, but on November 11 US forces arrested him and held him for the length of the siege. Al-Saadi's detention has been condemned by Reporters Without Borders and the International Federation of Journalists. 'We cannot ignore the possibility that he is being intimidated for just trying to do his job,' the IFJ stated. It's not the first time journalists in Iraq have faced this kind of intimidation. When US forces invaded Baghdad in April 2003, US Central Command urged all unembedded journalists to leave the city. Some insisted on staying and at least three paid with their lives. On April 8, a US aircraft bombed Al-Jazeera's Baghdad offices, killing reporter Tareq Ayyoub.

Al-Jazeera has documentation proving it gave the coordinates of its location to US forces. On the same day, a US tank fired on the Palestine hotel, killing José Couso, of the Spanish network Telecinco, and Taras Protsiuk, of Reuters. Three US soldiers are facing a criminal lawsuit from Couso's family, which alleges that US forces were well aware that journalists were in the Palestine hotel and that they committed a war crime.

US authorities have denied that hundreds of civilians were killed during last April's siege, and have lashed out at the sources of these reports. For instance, an unnamed 'senior American officer', speaking to the *New York Times* last month, labelled Fallujah general hospital 'a centre of propaganda'. But the strongest words were reserved for Arab TV networks.

Dahr Jamail

Although most of Sasha's dialogue is based on reports and testimonies collected by Dahr Jamail, it is not exclusively so.

Dahr Jamail is one of the few independent US journalists in Iraq. In an effort to expose the realities of the war in Iraq, his website (www.dahrjamailiraq.com/) relays the shocking testimonies of countless Iraqi civilians. These hard-hitting news stories have been translated into French, Polish, German, Dutch, Spanish, Japanese, Portuguese, Chinese, Arabic and Turkish. Dahr writes for the Inter Press Service and the *Asia Times*, and has had his reports published with such newspapers as the *Nation*, the *Sunday Herald*, Islam Online, the *Guardian* and the *Independent*. He also reports for Democracy Now!, the BBC, and several other internationally recognized radio and television stations. Over the course of his eight years in occupied Iraq, Dahr Jamail has authored a considerable amount of the resources cited in Fallujah.

3 April 2004

www.dahrjamailiraq.com/weblog/archives/
dispatches/000050.php

From Amman, on Fallujah

Amman, Jordan – By now I imagine everyone has been properly inundated with the images of the scorched bodies of the 'American Civilians' (as properly parroted by the corporate media) in Fallujah. In case I missed it before departing, I had one last chance to catch it on the countless televisions in JFK airport, then on the front page of the *NY Times* on the plane.

I thought it was interesting, because what accompanied this story was a strange little phenomenon I've seen many times in Iraq. The first bit of news released on the attack referred to the men killed as 'contractors', and even showed an Iraqi man handling the dog tags of one of them, and another man was holding a Department of Defense badge from another of the US fighters the Iraqis had killed. The same report mentioned that a collection of weapons was in one of the vehicles as well.

Of course that was the last of that footage I saw. From then on, it was 'Americans killed by Iraqis!', or 'Contractors Killed', over and over ad nauseum.

Well, it turns out these 'Americans killed by Iraqis' just happened to be four mercenaries working for a N.C. Security Firm called Blackwater Security Consulting.

This subcontractor, along with countless others, is working to provide 'security' in Iraq. Check out their website: because they even provide training for SWAT teams and former special operations personnel.

I've been in Fallujah when the entire city has been under collective punishment, which occurs nearly everytime someone attacks a US patrol there. People are enraged, and rightly so. So when one of those white, shiny SUVs with the big black antenna drives by with guys with crew cuts in them wearing body armor holding guns (yes, it is THAT obvious and easy to see), what do you think might happen to them?

The other reason I bring this up is because of this: Last night I'm going through customs at the airport in Amman, and I find myself standing in line behind five men with crewcuts and their 'handler', a little bit older fellow from Turkey (I saw his passport). The men were all in their late twenties, to late thirties I'd say, and from their discussion had all been in Iraq before.

They wouldn't tell me who they were working for, but when they were lugging huge plastic boxes with locks on them off the baggage belt, then went and hopped into their nice, white SUV, it was pretty much a no-brainer.

Blackwater Security Consulting won a $35.7 million contract to train over 10,000 soldiers from several states in the US in the art of 'force protection,' according to *Mother Jones* magazine. They also hire mercenaries from South Africa and other countries as well, and the pay in Iraq is $1,000 per day. Wonder how that makes our soldiers feel, who make barely over that each month?

So the residents of Fallujah are about to be 'pacified' because some of the resistance fighters there killed what were most likely mercenaries who regularly attack and detain residents of Fallujah. The fog of war grows thicker in Iraq, as the privatization contracts continue to be signed.

11 May, 2004

www.dahrjamailiraq.com/weblog/archives/dispatches/

Atrocities Continue to Emerge from the Rubble of Fallujah

One of the neighbors, seeing that I was a journalist, comes out to tell yet another horrific tale.

His brother, Hussein Mohammad Jergi was a forty-three-year-old man who had a mental disability. He wandered out of his home on the same day the car was shot and was shot and injured by the snipers.

With tears in his eyes, his brother angrily told the rest of the story. 'He was shot and ran into the house. They followed him into our home, took out a big knife and chopped off his feet. Then they shot him in the head. After destroying much of our furniture, and putting shit around my house, they left. This is how they behaved all over Fallujah. We buried my brother's feet with his body.'

15 November 2004

www.dahrjamailiraq.com/weblog/archives/
2004_11_14.php

Dogs Eating Bodies in the Streets of Fallujah

The horrendous humanitarian disaster of Fallujah drags on as the US military continues to refuse the entry of an Iraqi Red Crescent (IRC) convoy of relief supplies. The Red Crescent has appealed to the UN to intervene, but no such luck, nor does the military relent.

IPs [Iraqi Police], who are under US control, have looted Fallujah General Hospital. The military stopped the Red Crescent at the gates of the city and are not allowing them in. They allowed some bodies to be buried, but others are being eaten by dogs and cats in the streets, as reported by refugees just out of the city, as well as residents still trapped there.

The military said it saw no need for the IRC to deliver aid to people inside Fallujah because it did not think any civilians were still inside the city. Contradicting this claim, along with virtually every aid work, refugee, and resident of Fallujah was US Marine Colonel Mike Shupp who said, 'There is no need to bring [Red Crescent] supplies in because we have supplies of our own for the people.'

IRC spokeswoman Firdu al-Ubadi added, 'We know of at least 157 families inside Fallujah who need our help.'

23 November 2004

www.dahrjamailiraq.com/weblog/archives/dispatches/000136.php

Fallujah Refugees

'...I can't describe the situation in Fallujah and the condition of the people – Fallujah is suffering too much, it is almost gone now.'

He then explains, 'We got some supplies from the good people of Baghdad, and some volunteer doctors came on their own with some medicines, but they ran out daily because conditions are so bad. We saw nothing from the Ministry of Health – no medicines or doctors or anything.'

18 January 2005

www.dahrjamailiraq.com/weblog/archives/000173.php

Odd Happenings in Fallujah

'The soldiers are doing strange things in Fallujah,' said one of my contacts in Fallujah who just returned. He was in his city checking on his home and just returned to Baghdad this evening.

Speaking on condition of anonymity he continued, 'In the center of the Julan Quarter they are removing entire homes which have been bombed, meanwhile most of the

homes that were bombed are left as they were. Why are
they doing this?'

According to him, this was also done in the Nazal,
Mualmeen, Jubail and Shuhada'a districts, and the military
began to do this after Eid, which was after 20 November.

He told me he has watched the military use bulldozers
to push the soil into piles and load it onto trucks to carry
away. This was done in the Julan and Jimouriya quarters
of the city, which is of course where the heaviest fighting
occurred during the siege, as this was where resistance was
the fiercest.

'At least two kilometers of soil were removed,' he
explained, 'Exactly as they did at Baghdad Airport after
the heavy battles there during the invasion and the Americans used their special weapons.'

He explained that in certain areas where the military
used 'special munitions' 200 square meters of soil was
being removed from each blast site.

In addition, many of his friends have told him that the
military brought in water tanker trucks to power blast the
streets, although he hadn't seen this himself.

'They went around to every house and have shot the
water tanks,' he continued, 'As if they are trying to hide
the evidence of chemical weapons in the water, but they
only did this in some areas, such as Julan and in the *souk*
(market) there as well.'

He first saw this having been done after 20 December.

Again, this is reflective of stories I've been told by several
refugees from Fallujah.

Just last December, a thirty-five-year-old merchant from
Fallujah, Abu Hammad, told me what he'd experienced
when he was still in the city during the siege.

'The American warplanes came continuously through the night and bombed everywhere in Fallujah! It did not stop even for a moment! If the American forces did not find a target to bomb, they used sound bombs just to terrorize the people and children. The city stayed in fear; I cannot give a picture of how panicked everyone was.'

'In the mornings I found Fallujah empty, as if nobody lives in it,' he'd said, 'Even poisonous gases have been used in Fallujah – they used everything – tanks, artillery, infantry, poison gas. Fallujah has been bombed to the ground. Nothing is left.'

In Amiriyat al-Fallujah, a small city just outside Fallujah where many doctors from Fallujah have been practicing since they were unable to do so at Fallujah General Hospital, similar stories are being told.

Last month one refugee who had just arrived at the hospital in the small city explained that he'd watched the military bring in water tanker trucks to power blast some of the streets in Fallujah.

'Why are they doing this,' explained Ahmed (name changed for his protection), 'To beautify Fallujah? No! They are covering their tracks from the horrible weapons they used in my city.'

Also last November, another Fallujah refugee from the Julan area, Abu Sabah told me, 'They (US military) used these weird bombs that put up smoke like a mushroom cloud. Then small pieces feel [fell] from the air with long tails of smoke behind them.'

He explained that pieces of these bombs exploded into large fires that burnt people's skin even when water was dumped on their bodies, which is the effect of phosphorus weapons, as well as napalm. 'People suffered so much from these, both civilians and fighters alike,' he said.

My friend Suthir (name changed to protect identity) was a member of one of the Iraqi Red Crescent relief convoys that was allowed into Fallujah at the end of November.

'I'm sure the Americans committed bad things there, but who can discover and say this,' she said when speaking of what she saw of the devastated city, 'They didn't allow us to go to the Julan area or any of the others where there was heavy fighting, and I'm sure that is where the horrible things took place.'

'The Americans didn't let us in the places where everyone said there was napalm used,' she added, 'Julan and those places where the heaviest fighting was, nobody is allowed to go there.'

On 30 November the US military prevented an aid convoy from reaching Fallujah. This aid convoy was sent by the Iraqi Ministry of Health, but was told by soldiers at a checkpoint to return in 'eight or nine days', reported AP.

Dr Ibrahim al-Kubaisi who was with the relief team told reporters at that time, 'There is a terrible crime going in Fallujah and they do not want anybody to know.'

With the military maintaining strict control over who enters Fallujah, the truth of what weapons were used remains difficult to find.

Meanwhile, people who lived in different districts of Fallujah continue to tell the same stories.

8 February 2005

www.dahrjamailiraq.com/weblog/archives/
dispatches/000196.php

Stories from Fallujah

These are the stories that will continue to emerge from the rubble of Fallujah for years. No, for generations...

Speaking on condition of anonymity, the doctor sits with me in a hotel room in Amman, where he is now a refugee. He'd spoken about what he saw in Fallujah in the UK, and now is under threat by the US military if he returns to Iraq.

'I started speaking about what happened in Fallujah during both sieges in order to raise awareness, and the Americans raided my house three times,' he says, talking so fast I can barely keep up. He is driven to tell what he's witnessed, and as a doctor working inside Fallujah, he has video and photographic proof of all that he tells me.

'I entered Fallujah with a British medical and humanitarian convoy at the end of December, and stayed until the end of January,' he explains. 'But I was in Fallujah before that to work with people and see what their needs were, so I was in there since the beginning of December [2004].'

When I ask him to explain what he saw when he first entered Fallujah in December he says it was like a tsunami struck the city.

'Fallujah is surrounded by refugee camps where people are living in tents and old cars,' he explains, 'It reminded me of Palestinian refugees. I saw children coughing because of the cold and there are no medicines. Most everyone left their houses with nothing, and no money, so how can they live depending only on humanitarian aid?'

The doctors says that in one refugee camp in the northern area of Fallujah there were 1,200 students living in seven tents.

'The disaster caused by this siege is so much worse than the first one, which I witnessed first hand,' he says, and then tells me he'll use one story as an example.

'One story is of a young girl who is sixteen years old,' he says of one of the testimonies he video taped recently, 'She stayed for three days with the bodies of her family who were killed in their home. When the soldiers entered she was in her home with her father, mother, twelve-year-old brother and two sisters. She watched the soldiers enter and shoot her mother and father directly, without saying anything.'

The girl managed to hide behind the refrigerator with her brother and witnessed the war crimes first-hand.

'They beat her two sisters, then shot them in the head,' he said. After this her brother was enraged and ran at the soldiers while shouting at them, so they shot him dead.

'She continued hiding after the soldiers left and stayed with her sisters because they were bleeding, but still alive. She was too afraid to call for help because she feared the soldiers would come back and kill her as well. She stayed for three days, with no water and no food, with the dead bodies of her family around her. Eventually one of the American snipers saw her and took her to the hospital,' he added before reminding me again that he had all of her testimony documented on film.

He briefly told me of another story he documented of a mother who was in her home during the siege. 'On the fifth day of the siege her home was bombed, and the roof fell on her son, cutting his legs off, he says while using his hands to make cutting motions on his legs, 'For hours she couldn't go outside because they announced that anyone going in the street would be shot. So all she could do was wrap his legs and watch him die before her eyes.'

He pauses for a few deep breaths, then continues, 'All I can say is that Fallujah is like it was struck by a tsunami. There weren't many families in there after the siege, but they had absolutely nothing. The suffering was beyond what you can imagine. When the Americans finally let us in people were fighting just for a blanket.'

'One of my colleagues, Dr Saleh Alsawi, he was speaking so angrily about them. He was in the main hospital when they raided it at the beginning of the siege. They entered the theater room when they were working on a patient...he was there because he's an anaesthesiologist. They entered with their boots on, beat the doctors and took them out, leaving the patient on the table to die.'

This story has already been reported in the Arab media.

The doctor tells me of the bombing of the Hay Nazal clinic during the first week of the siege.

'This contained all the foreign aid and medical instruments we had. All the US military commanders knew this, because we told them about it so they wouldn't bomb it. But this was one of the clinics bombed, and in the first week of the siege they bombed it two times.'

He then adds, 'Of course they targeted all our ambulances and doctors. Everyone knows this.'

The doctor tells me he and some other doctors are trying to sue the US military for the following incident, for which he has the testimonial evidence on tape.

It is a story I was told by several refugees in Baghdad as well…at the end of last November while the siege was still in progress.

'During the second week of the siege they entered and announced that all the families have to leave their homes and meet at an intersection in the street while carrying a white flag. They gave them seventy-two hours to leave and after that they would be considered an enemy,' he says.

'We documented this story with video a family of twelve, including a relative and his oldest child who was seven years old. They heard this instruction, so they left with all their food and money they could carry, and white flags. When they reached the intersection where the families were accumulating, they heard someone shouting "Now!" in English, and shooting started everywhere.'

The family was all carrying white flags, as instructed, according to the young man who gave his testimony. Yet he watched his mother and father shot by snipers – his mother in the head and his father shot in the heart. His two aunts were shot, then his brother was shot in the neck. The man stated that when he raised himself from the ground to shout for help, he was shot in the side.

'After some hours he raised his arm for help and they shot his arm,' continues the doctor, 'So after awhile he raised his hand and they shot his hand.'

A six-year-old boy of the family was standing over the bodies of his parents, crying, and he too was then shot.

'Anyone who raised up was shot,' adds the doctor, then added again that he had photographs of the dead as well as photos of the gunshot wounds of the survivors.

'Once it grew dark some of them along with this man who spoke with me, with his child and sister-in-law and sister managed to crawl away after it got dark. They crawled to a building and stayed for eight days. They had one cup of water and gave it to the child. They used cooking oil to put on their wounds which were of course infected, and found some roots and dates to eat.'

He stops here. His eyes look around the room as cars pass by outside on wet streets ... water hissing under their tires.

He left Fallujah at the end of January, so I ask him what it was like when he left recently.

'Now maybe 25 per cent of the people have returned, but there are still no doctors. The hatred now of Fallujans against every American is incredible, and you cannot blame them. The humiliation at the checkpoints is only making people even angrier,' he tells me.

'I've been there, and I saw that anyone who even turns their head is threatened and hit by both American and Iraqi soldiers alike ... one man did this, and when the Iraqi soldier tried to humiliate him, the man took a gun of a nearby soldier and killed two ING [Iraqi National Guard], so then of course he was shot.'

The doctor tells me they are keeping people in the line for several hours at a time, in addition to the US military making propaganda films of the situation.

'And I've seen them use the media – and on 2 January at the north checkpoint in the north part of Fallujah, they were giving people $200 per family to return to Fallujah so they can film them in the line...when actually, at that time, nobody was returning to Fallujah,' he says. It reminds me of the story my colleague told me of what he saw in January. At that time a CNN crew was escorted in by the military to film street cleaners that were brought in as props, and soldiers handing out candy to children.

'You must understand the hatred that has been caused…
it has gotten more difficult for Iraqis, including myself, to
make the distinction between the American government
and the American people,' he tells me.

His story is like countless others.

'My cousin was a poor man in Fallujah,' he explains,
'He walked from his house to work and back, while living
with his wife and five daughters. In July of 2003, American soldiers entered his house and woke them all up. They
drug [dragged] them into the main room of the house,
and executed my cousin in front of his family. Then they
simply left.'

He pauses then holds up his hands and asks, 'Now, how
are these people going to feel about Americans?'

28 April 2005

www.democracynow.org/article.
pl?sid=05/04/28/1346252

Iraq Through the Eyes of Unembedded, Independent Journalist Dahr Jamail

*Dahr Jamail, one of the few independent, unembedded
journalists reporting in Iraq for months, joins us in our
firehouse studio to discuss the siege of Fallujah, detention
of Iraqis, so-called 'reconstruction' and much more.*

Fallujah, which was the symbol of the resistance in Iraq
to the US occupation and throughout the Middle East
at that point is now 70% estimated to be bombed to the
ground, no water, no electricity. People who want to go
back into that city have to get retina scans, all ten fingers

fingerprinted, then they're issued an ID card. People inside the city are referring to it as a big jail. It is a horrendous situation, and we still have hundreds of thousands of refugees as a result. And the goal of the mission of [be]sieging Fallujah as announced by the US military was to capture the phantom Zarqawi and to bring security and stability for the elections, and what's left is a situation where Fallujah is in shambles, and the resistance has spread throughout the country.

Eliot Weinberger

What I heard about Iraq

What I heard about Iraq – put together by poet and critic Eliot Weinberger – is a chronologically organized compilation of government pledges, allegations, speculations, revenge tactics, defending statements and more; it is a staggeringly revealing compendium of the reports dispatched by the media. A stage adaptation of the essay – written by Simon Levy – is set to be performed to commemorate the third anniversary of the invasion of Iraq. The readings, coordinated by the Fountain Theatre, in association with the internationales literaturfestival Berlin (www.literaturfestival. com/news1_3_2_496.html) and the Peter Weiss Foundation for Art and Politics, will take place on an international scale. In addition to this Levy has written three extra renditions of the piece which the Fountain Theatre has made available to theatres, schools, advocacy groups and human rights organizations worldwide. Please refer to www.fountaintheatre. com/WorldwideReadingofWHATIHEARDABOUTIRAQ. htm for more information. *What I heard about Iraq* has been published as a book by Verso, and is also available to read on the *London Review of Books* website. Here are some excerpts from the document

I heard an American soldier say: 'There's a picture of the World Trade Center hanging up by my bed and I keep one in my Kevlar. Every time I feel sorry for these people I look at that. I think: "They hit us at home and now it's our turn."'

And when the National Museum was emptied and the National Library burned down, I heard him say: 'The images you are seeing on television you are seeing over, and over, and over, and it's the same picture of some person walking out of some building with a vase, and you see it twenty times, and you think: "My goodness, were there that many vases? Is it possible that there were that many vases in the whole country?"'

...

I heard the US was building fourteen 'enduring bases', capable of housing 110,000 soldiers, and I heard Brigadier-General Mark Kimmitt call them 'a blueprint for how we could operate in the Middle East'. I heard that the US was building what would be its largest embassy anywhere in the world.

I heard that it would only be a matter of months before Starbucks and McDonald's opened branches in Baghdad. I heard that HSBC would have cash machines all over the country.

I heard about the trade fairs run by New Bridges Strategies, a consulting firm that promised access to the Iraqi market. I heard one of its partners say: 'Getting the rights to distribute Procter & Gamble would be a gold mine. One well-stocked 7-Eleven could knock out thirty Iraqi stores. A Wal-Mart could take over the country.'

...

I heard Richard Perle tell Americans to 'relax and celebrate victory'. I heard him say: 'The predictions of those who opposed this war can be discarded like spent cartridges.'

I heard Lieutenant-General Jay Garner say: 'We ought to look in a mirror and get proud and stick out our chests and suck in our bellies and say: "Damn, we're Americans."'...

...

I heard that the US, as a gift from the American people to the Iraqi people, had committed $18.4 billion to the reconstruction of basic infrastructure, but that future Iraqi governments would have no say in how the money was spent. I heard that the economy had been opened to foreign ownership, and that this could not be changed. I heard that the Iraqi army would be under the command of the US, and that this could not be changed. I heard, however, that 'full authority' for health and hospitals had been turned over to the Iraqis, and that senior American health advisers had been withdrawn. I heard Tommy Thompson, Secretary of Health and Human Services, say that Iraq's hospitals would be fine if the Iraqis 'just washed their hands and cleaned the crap off the walls'.

...

I heard Colonel Nathan Sassaman say: 'With a heavy dose of fear and violence, and a lot of money for projects, I think we can convince these people that we are here to help them.'

...

I heard Donald Rumsfeld say: 'Death has a tendency to encourage a depressing view of war.'

...

I heard a Marine commander tell his men: 'You will be held accountable for the facts not as they are in hindsight but as they appeared to you at the time. If, in your mind, you fire to protect yourself or your men, you are doing the right thing. It doesn't matter if later on we find out you wiped out a family of unarmed civilians.'

...

I heard Lieutenant-Colonel Mark Smith say: 'We're going out where the bad guys live, and we're going to slay them in their zip code.'

...

I heard that 5 per cent of eligible voters had registered for the coming elections.

I heard General John Abizaid say: 'I don't think Iraq will have a perfect election. And, if I recall, looking back at our own election four years ago, it wasn't perfect either.'

I heard Donald Rumsfeld say: 'Let's say you tried to have an election and you could have it in three-quarters or four-fifths of the country. But some places you couldn't because the violence is too great. Well, so be it. Nothing's perfect in life.'

I heard an Iraqi engineer say: 'Go and vote and risk being blown to pieces or followed by insurgents and murdered for co-operating with the Americans? For what? To prac-tise democracy? Are you joking?'

...

I heard that Spain left the 'coalition of the willing'. Hungary left; the Dominican Republic left; Nicaragua left; Honduras left. I heard that the Philippines had left early, after a Filipino truck driver was kidnapped and executed. Norway left. Poland and the Netherlands said they were leaving. Thailand said it was leaving. Bulgaria was reduc-ing its few hundred troops. Moldova cut its force from forty-two to twelve.

I heard that the president had once said: 'Two years from now, only the Brits may be with us. At some point, we may be the only ones left. That's OK with me. We are America.'

Condoleezza Rice

16 October 2001

www.whitehouse.gov/news/releases/2001/10/
20011016- 3.html

For Immediate Release. Office of the Press Secretary

National Security Advisor's Interview with Al-Jazeera TV
Old Executive Office Building, 2:34 P.M. EDT

Q: (Introduction in Arabic) Dr Rice, we would like to thank you very much for this opportunity that you give to Al-Jazeera and to our audience in the Arab and Muslim world. And since we have a limited time, let me start first with the latest developments.

British Prime Minister Blair met with Chairman Arafat. They both emphasized the importance of reviving the peace process. Chairman Arafat called on the Israeli government to start immediately the permanent status negotiations. Would you second him in that appeal?

DR RICE: Thank you very much for the opportunity to be with you. Indeed, we took note of the very fruitful discussions between Prime Minister Blair and Chairman Arafat. The United States fully agrees that as soon as possible we should get into the Mitchell Process, which lays out a road map toward meaningful political negotiations toward a final status.

...

Q: If we move to the current crisis that started September 11th and, of course, the military actions since last Sunday. We see from polls and from demonstrations in the street that while governments support the US, the public on the streets in the Arab and Muslim world do not [do that]. Do you think that there is a problem because the US only rely on government support, regardless of [what] the people [think]?

DR RICE: We, of course, have very good relations with a number of governments in the Middle East. But we care very much also about the people of the Middle East, the Arab populations. And the United States is a place to which many Arabs have looked as a place – we have a number of Arab immigrants in the United States.

I was a professor at Stanford University; the largest growing population of Stanford University was the Muslim student population. We think that the United States is a place in which religious tolerance and a belief that all people should live together in peace is a message that would resonate with populations in the region. And so we're trying to do a better job in getting that message out to people. We want it to be very clear that the war on terrorism is not a war against Islam. Islam is a peaceful religion. Islam is a religion that respects innocent human life.

So we cannot believe that Islam would countenance the kind of destruction of innocence that we saw on September 11th. Many Muslims in the United States lost their lives in those bombings.

So our view is that the populations – we believe that there is still a reservoir of goodwill for the United States that we can tap into. We are concerned about the economic prosperity and opportunity for people in the Middle East. And that's a message that we will continue to carry.

Q: So is it a problem of perception, an image of the US only, or is it policies that are perceived to be double standards and we need to review the US policies in the Middle East? Are we reviewing it or things going to stay the same only – in public relation arena will be more active?

DR RICE: No, we believe that the policies that the United States is pursuing are ones that are good for the Middle East as a whole – populations that are Arab populations, as well as the population of Israel.

A viable peace process that leads to the kind of world that the President has talked about – with a Palestinian state and an Israeli state that live together in peace, where Israel can live in peace with her neighbors – this would be good for the whole region. And it's been the policy of the United States now for years to pursue that.

We have pursued economic development with close partners in the region. We just signed a free trade agreement with Jordan that we believe will bring jobs and opportunity to the population of Jordan. We have a healthy economic dialogue with Egypt. We think that our policies are policies that are healthy for the region. And as so, we look forward to talking more about the policies. This is not just a matter of perception; it is a matter of policies that we think are healthy for the region.

Q: Aside from the Arab-Israeli conflict that you talked about – and that seems that the US policy is not going to change in that regard – Iraq, as you might have heard in many of the tapes of bin Laden or others, or even other people [who] aren't friends of the US, is one of the sources of friction or problems for people in the Middle East toward US policy. However, you are personally perceived as one of the few people in the administration who would like to enlarge the war in terrorism to include Iraq. Correct me, please.

DR RICE: Iraq has been a problem not just for US policy, but for policy in the region, as well. This is a country that could not even acknowledge the right to exist of Kuwait. This is a country that has threatened its neighbors, that has been harmful to its own people.

And we believe that our policies toward Iraq simply are to protect the region and to protect Iraq's people and neighbors.

Now, we understood when we came to power here in Washington several months ago that we had a problem, for instance, on Iraqi sanctions; that people believed, or that Saddam Hussein was claiming, that the sanctions that were in place were somehow harming the Iraqi people. We do not believe that they were harming the Iraqi people because in the north, where the UN administers the oil-for-food program, Iraqi people are doing well. It's only where Saddam Hussein administers oil-for-food that there is a problem with the Iraqi people.

But that said, we want to change the sanctions. We want to change the sanctions so that they are aimed at the regime, which is a danger to its neighbors, not at the people.

Q: Other than that, there is no military action awaiting Iraq after all the military mobilization in the area as a second stage of this war on terrorism?

DR RICE: The President has made very clear that the war on terrorism is a broad war on terrorism. You can't be for terrorism in one part of the world and against it in another part of the world. We worry about Saddam Hussein. We worry about his weapons of mass destruction that he's trying to achieve.

There's a reason he doesn't want UN inspectors – it's because he intends to acquire weapons of mass destruction. But for now, the President has said that his goal is to watch and monitor Iraq; and, certainly, the United States will act if Iraq threatens its interests.

Q: How about Syria?

DR RICE: With Syria, we've been very clear that we do not believe that Syria can be against al Qaida, but in favor of other terrorist groups. But we have had some discussions with Syria. The President, in his speech to the Joint Session, said: those who continue to harbor terrorists. That's an invitation to countries to stop the practice of harboring terrorism.

Q: So if Syria does not cooperate against people who are from Jihad or Hamas, they should be targeted also?

DR RICE: We have ruled out at this point issues that concern making – that draw distinctions between types of terrorism. We just don't think that's the right thing to do. You can't say there are good terrorists and there are bad terrorists. But the means that we use with different countries to get them to stop harboring terrorists may be very broad. And there are many means at our disposal.

Right now, our discussions with Syria, which are not – there are not a lot of discussions with Syria, but we have had discussions with Syria that suggest: get out of the business of sponsoring terrorism. We're asking that of every state of the world. You cannot be neutral in this fight; you either are for terrorism or against it.

Q: Dr Rice, you met recently with executives, or at least in a conference call with executives of US networks [to ask them] not to tape, not to broadcast, or at least review bin Laden's tapes or anything coming from Kabul. It has been perceived in the Arab world as censorship. What is your answer to that?

DR RICE: My answer to that is that the discussions with the network executives were very fruitful, and I think they have been very responsible, because they understood that having a fifteen-minute or 20-minute tape that was pre-taped, prerecorded, that sat there and did nothing but incite hatred and, ultimately, attacks against innocent Americans was not a matter of news, it was a matter of propaganda, and it was inciting attacks against Americans.

Now, I understand that Al-Jazeera has guidelines of its own on how to handle a tape like this, and we applaud that you would have guidelines of this kind, because what we do not need is to have a kind of free rein to sit and use the airwaves to incite attacks on innocent people.

Q: Overall, how do you perceive Al-Jazeera as a credible or independent media? And should US government officials encourage that, or try to influence government of Qatar in order to crack down in the only – what are perceived to be the only independent media in the region?

DR RICE: Well, if I did not have respect for Al-Jazeera, I would not be doing this interview.

Q: Thank you.

DR RICE: I think it's important that there be a network that reaches broad Arab audiences. And the United States believes in freedom of the press. We believe that the press is one of the most fundamental bases for democracy and for individuals to have the kind of dignity that human beings should have. And so I'm delighted to be here on Al-Jazeera. I know that you're going to have many of my colleagues on in the future, and I look forward to being back with you.

Q: Thank you. And I leave you at the end just with a statement from you without my interference, to our audience in the Arab and Muslim world, whatever you would like to tell them.

DR RICE: I would like to say to the Arab and Muslim world the following. I would like to say that America is a country that respects religious difference. America is a country that has many people of different religions within it. The fastest-growing religion in America is the Muslim faith.

The President of the United States has said that our war on terrorism is not a war against Islam. It is not a war against the Arab people. It is a war against evil people who would hijack the Palestinian cause.

As Yasser Arafat said today, there is no connection between what al Qaida does and the Palestinian cause. It is a war against people who take the lives of innocents willingly in terrorist attacks against office buildings or against the Pentagon.

This is a war against the evil of terrorism. The President of the United States understands Islam to be a faith of peace, a faith that protects innocents, and the policy of the United States is to do the same.

Thank you very much.

Q: Thank you, Dr Rice.

END 2:50 P.M. EDT

29 April 2002

www.whitehouse.gov/news/releases/2002/04/
20020429-9.html

For Immediate Release. Office of the Press Secretary

Remarks by National Security Advisor Condoleezza Rice on Terrorism and Foreign Policy, Paul H. Nitze School of Advanced International Studies, Johns Hopkins University, Kennedy Auditorium, Washington, DC 12:00 P.M.

It's going to take years to understand the long-term effects of September 11th. But even now we are beginning to recognize that there are certain verities that September 11th reinforced and brought home to us in the most vivid way.

First, there has been an end to innocence about international politics and about our own vulnerability. We see that wars of consequence are not mere relics of a bygone era. We see that in years to come the primary energies of America's Armed Forces will be devoted to more than just managing civil conflict and humanitarian assistance.

As the world's most powerful nation, the United States has a special responsibility to help make the world more secure. And when we were attacked on September 11th, it reinforced one of the rediscovered truths about today's world: robust military power matters in international politics and in security.

Second, the events of September 11th underscored the idea that a sound foreign policy begins at home. We are now engaged in trying to harden the country. That means thinking about airport security, visa requirements, protection of nuclear power plants and other physical and cyber security infrastructure.

We also are working with the American Armed Forces to make certain that the role of America's Armed Forces, in defending our territory, our airspace, our land and our sea, is properly taken care of. And that is why Secretary Rumsfeld and Chairman Myers have proposed the creation of a US Northern Command – having America's Armed Forces cover for the first time the American continent, wholly consistent with American constitutional responsibilities and expectations, but with a new understanding that America's frontiers need to be safe.

In doing so, we recognize that we have to secure our own neighborhood, not just America's borders. And we are now cooperating with Mexico and Canada in unprecedented ways to construct smart and modern borders – borders that protect us from those who would harm us, but facilitate the trade and human interchange that enrich us.

Since the earliest days of the campaign for President, President Bush has stated his determination to build a fully democratic Western hemisphere that lives and trades in freedom and grows in prosperity. Strong, prosperous neighbors export their goods, not their problems – like drugs and terror.

The third truth is that we can only do so much to protect ourselves at home, and so the best defense is a good offense. We have to take the fight to the terrorists. And that means that there can be no distinction between terrorists and those who harbor them. So in addition to pursuing al Qaida, we have also pursued the Taliban and the government of Afghanistan, as we knew that they had shared responsibilities for the terrorist attacks.

Now with the Taliban out of power and al Qaida damaged, we have moved into the second stage of our war on terror. But let's be very clear: much remains to be done in Afghanistan. Ultimately, Afghanistan will be secured by more democracy and more prosperity. This great project is not America's alone and it will require a broad range of tools. We need to help Afghanistan build up its political institutions, its economic institutions and its civil society. Building a nation is not an American military task – it is a joint project, a long-term project between the Afghan people and the international community.

Beyond Afghanistan, we are engaged in a sustained campaign to deny sanctuary to terrorists, regardless of where they are from and where they commit their crimes. Our message to every leader on every continent is that terrorism can support no cause, it is never, never legitimate; it is, by its very nature, evil; terrorists have no positive agenda; terrorists are not for anything, they are against peace and freedom and life itself.

Recent events in the Middle East illustrate the terrible damage, the terrible toll of terrorism. Innocent lives are being lost. People who could be living together in peace are being driven apart by death and destruction. And on April 4th, the President called on all parties – Israel, the

Palestinians and regional leaders among the Arab neighbors – to accept their responsibilities to create an environment free from violence and terror.

A fourth truth that September 11th underscored was the need to deny terrorists and hostile states the opportunity to acquire weapons of mass destruction. The world's most dangerous people simply cannot be permitted to obtain the world's most dangerous weapons. And it is a stubborn and extremely troubling fact that the list of states that sponsor terror and the lists of states that are seeking to acquire weapons of mass destruction overlap substantially.

We do not see how these facts can be denied. And if these facts are admitted, they must be confronted. We must use every tool at our disposal to meet this grave global threat, including strengthened non-proliferation regimes and export controls, and moving ahead with missile defense to deny any benefit to those who would try and acquire weapons of mass destruction.

The United States and our coalition partners must act deliberately. But inaction is not an option. As the President has said, we must not and we will not wait on events while dangers gather.

Finally, the new challenges have underscored the critical importance of allies, partners and coalitions. Global terror demands a global solution. Right now there are twenty countries with forces operating in and around Afghanistan, one of the largest military coalitions assembled since the Gulf War. And there are many who are not a part of the military coalition who are providing important intelligence, law enforcement and efforts to cut off terrorist financing.

In this we have been tremendously helped by our allies around the world. And our NATO allies have particularly led the way, especially Britain, which heads the International Security Assistance Force for Afghanistan and has sent air and naval and special forces into the region. America will never forget that within twenty-four hours of the attacks, NATO, for the first time in its history, invoked Article V of its charter, stating that an attack on one is an attack on all.

We will continue to work closely with our friends and our allies as the war progresses and as we seek victory over the scourge of terrorism.

These enduring truths, made more vivid by September 11th, are very important to centering our foreign policy. But there is one other important truth from this period: an earthquake of the magnitude of 9/11 can shift the tectonic plates of international politics. The international system has been in flux since the collapse of Soviet power. Now it is possible – indeed, probable – that that transition is coming to an end.

If that is right, if the collapse of the Soviet Union and 9/11 bookend a major shift in international politics, then this is a period not just of grave danger, but of enormous opportunity. Before the clay is dry again, America and our friends and our allies must move decisively to take advantage of these new opportunities. This is, then, a period akin to 1945 to 1947, when American leadership expanded the number of free and democratic states – Japan and Germany among the great powers – to create a new balance of power that favored freedom.

It is, indeed, possible to see age-old problems in a new light. And, as an academic, may I suggest, to put aside age-old distinctions between realism and neoliberalism in thinking about the task ahead. Put more simply than any of its proponents would find acceptable, realists downplay the importance of values and the internal structures of states, emphasizing instead the balance of power as the key to stability and peace. Neoliberals emphasize the primacy of values, such as freedom and democracy and human rights and institutions, in ensuring that a just political order is obtained.

As a professor, I recognize that these debates enliven our conferences and our classrooms. (Laughter.) I have participated in them, myself. In fact, most of us got tenure because we participated in them. (Laughter.) But as a policymaker, I can tell you that they obscure reality. Power matters. Great powers matter. Great powers matter because they can influence international stability for good or for ill due their size, influence and their will. Great powers never have, and never will just mind their own business within their borders.

Thus, the Soviet Union's collapse was important both because it resolved a high-stakes struggle that profoundly affected world peace and security, but also because values and ideas, democracy, markets and freedom triumphed. The socialist alternative that had existed for seventy-plus years, which kept so much of the world isolated from the international economy and deprived so many millions of the benefits of freedom, died alongside the hammer and the sickle. Our goal today, then, is not just a favorable balance of power, but what President Bush has called a balance of power that favors freedom.

After the end of the Cold War, and still in the shadow of September 11th, we may well be on the cusp of an era in which the world will not be bedeviled by great power rivalry. There will be differences among the great powers. But if the scales tip toward shared interest, rather than interest in conflict between them, this will truly be an era unlike any other.

September 11th and its aftermath illuminated a fundamental divide between the forces of chaos and those of order. And all the world's great powers clearly see themselves as falling on the same side of this divide, and they are acting accordingly. Europe and the United States see that our common and fundamental interests and values far outweigh our differences. When people are trying to kill you, and when they attack because they hate freedom, other disputes – from Franken-food to bananas to even important issues like the environment – suddenly look a bit different. They look like policy differences, not fundamental clashes of values.

Germany and Japan have begun to adopt new security roles that correspond with their identities as leading powers and democracies. Russia's democratic transition is by no means yet complete. Yet, September 11th has helped to clarify elements of a common security agenda with Russia. We have also worked cooperatively on a range of issues with India, an emerging democratic power, even as we work closely with Pakistan. And we are optimistic about the future of our relationship with China, a country in the midst of a fundamental and still uncertain transition. But the emergence of a China that embraces the rule of law, markets and, ultimately, democracy would have a profound and positive effect on world security and prosperity.

A balance of power that favors freedom is, at its core, a balance of power based on the ascendancy of shared values on every continent. That is why in places such as Russia and China, values matter. They matter in our relations and they matter to the outcome of the balance of power that favors freedom – values like religious freedom, media freedom and a recognition of the aspirations of long-suffering minority groups. It is not enough for the great powers to share an interest in order; we need to move to sharing an interest in an order that is based on common values.

America today possesses as much power and influence as any nation or entity in the world, and certainly in history. But in stark contrast to the leading powers of centuries past, our ambitions are not territorial. Our military and economic power are complemented by and multiplied by the values that underpin them: democracy, freedom, human rights, the rule of law, honest government, respect for women and children, private property, free speech, equal justice and religious tolerance.

That is why America seeks a great world beyond the victory over terror. We seek not merely to leave the world safer, but to leave it better; to leave it a world that makes it possible for all men and women to experience the exhilaration and the challenges of freedom. This mission to leave the world safer and better is more important than ever in the face of September 11th. That is why President Bush is strongly committed to free trade as a cornerstone of American policy – trade that advances economic growth at home and abroad and advances the forces of freedom, as well.

That is why in Monterrey, Mexico, last month the President put forth a new compact for global development defined by greater resources from wealthy nations and greater responsibility from developing nations. That fund will benefit poor countries, especially in Africa, but also in Latin America. The President pledged to seek a 50 percent increase in America's core development assistance, with new funds devoted to projects and nations that govern justly, invest in their people and encourage economic freedom.

There is also a new urgency to address our relations with Muslim societies around the world in a positive way. This war in which we are engaged is not a clash of civilizations; it cannot be a clash of civilizations. Extremism and progress are most assuredly enemies of one another. But you do not have to reject tradition and belief to reap the benefits of integration into modern society.

This was the central insight of Pakistan President Musharraf's speech on January 12th. And as President Bush recognized in his speech, the State of the Union, all fathers and mothers in all societies want their children to be educated and live free from poverty and violence. The United States will stand with people on every continent, in Muslim societies and in all societies that seek to claim a better future for their people.

Education will play a particularly important role in societies that are making this quest. A good education teaches an appreciation of practical skills for the global economy. But is also provides a forum in which one learns to live with difference and to respect the rights of others. It fuels new hopes, instead of old hatreds.

Americans have a deep understanding of the ability of education to open you up to the full range of possibilities. At Stanford, I was always heartened to stand before a class in which a fourth-generation Stanford legatee sat next to the son or daughter of a migrant farm worker. It reinforced that education is the great equalizer. Because after that experience, it would not matter where they came from, it would matter where they were going.

Here at SAIS, there are not only diverse students from a collection of American families, but also people from different backgrounds and from different countries – some seventy nations. The common experience shared here by students, many of whom will go on to leadership roles here and in their own countries, will influence choices for a long, long time to come. And choices are important. Our continued success in the fight against terror, our success in making the world safer and better hinges on the choices made by the rest of the world.

America cannot impose its vision on the world – yet, we will use our influence to favor freedom. There are right and wrong choices and right and wrong acts. And governments are making them every day for their own people and for the people of the world. We can never let the intricacies of cloistered debate – with its many hues of gray and nuance – obscure the need to speak and act with moral clarity. We must recognize that some states or leaders will choose wrongly. We must recognize that truly evil regimes will never be reformed. And we must recognize that such regimes must be confronted, not coddled.

Nations must decide which side they are on in the fault line that divides civilization from terror. They must decide whether to embrace the paradigm of progress: democracy and freedom and human rights, and clean limited government. Together, with others, we can help people and nations make positive choices as they seek a better future, and we can deter those who want to take away a better future for others.

September 11th reintroduced America to a part of itself that some had forgotten, or that some thought we no longer had. We have been reminded that defending freedom was not just the work of the greatest generation, it is the work of every generation. And we will carry this better part of ourselves out into the wider world.

October 2002

www.banneroftruth.org/pages/articles/
article_detail.php?190

The Christian Testimony of Condoleezza Rice

Miss Condoleezza Rice (47) is the American National Security Advisor. She has reached the highest political office for an African-American woman to have attained. Her father was a Presbyterian minister and she was trained as a girl to be a concert pianist and a competitive ice skater. During an August 4 Sunday school class at the National Presbyterian Church, Washington, she explained something of her own faith in God. Here are some excerpts:

I was a preacher's kid, so Sundays were church, no doubt about that. The church was the center of our lives. In segregated black Birmingham of the late 1950s and early 1960s, the church was not just a place of worship. It was the place where families gathered; it was the social center of the community, too.

Although I never doubted the existence of God, I think, like all people I've had some ups and downs in my faith. When I first moved to California in 1981 to join the faculty at Stanford, there were a lot of years when I was not attending church regularly. I was traveling a lot. I was a specialist in international politics, so I was always traveling abroad. I was always in another time zone.

One Sunday I was in the Lucky's Supermarket not very far from my house – I will never forget – among the spices an African-American man walked up to me and said he was buying some things for his church picnic.

And he said, 'Do you play the piano by any chance?'

I said, 'Yes.' They said they were looking for someone to play the piano at church. It was a little African-American church right in the center of Palo Alto. A Baptist church. So I started playing for that church. That got me regularly back into churchgoing. I don't play gospel very well – I play Brahms – and you know how black ministers will start a song and the musicians will pick it up? I had no idea what I was doing and so I called my mother, who had played for Baptist churches.

'Mother,' I said, 'they just start. How am I supposed to do this?' She said, 'Honey, play in C and they'll come back to you.' And that's true. If you play in C, people will come back. I tell that story because I thought to myself 'My goodness, God has a long reach.' I mean, in the Lucky's Supermarket on a Sunday morning.

I played for about six months for them and then I decided to go and find the Presbyterian Church again. I'm a devoted Presbyterian. I really like the governance structure of the church. I care about the Presbyterian Church. On a Sunday morning, I went to Menlo Park Presbyterian Church in Palo Alto. The minister that Sunday morning gave a sermon I will never quite forget. It was about the Prodigal Son from the point of view of the elder son.

It set the elder son up not as somebody who had done all the right things but as somebody who had become so self-satisfied; a parable about self-satisfaction, and contentment and complacency in faith, [and] that people who didn't somehow expect themselves to need to be born again can be so complacent.

I started to think of myself as that elder son who had never doubted the existence of the Heavenly Father but wasn't really walking in faith in an active way any more.

I started to become more active with the church to go to Bible study and to have a more active prayer life. It was a very important turning point in my life.

My father was an enormous influence in my spiritual life. He was a theologian, a doctor of divinity. He was someone who let you argue about things. He didn't say, 'Just accept it.' And when I had questions, which we all do, he encouraged that.

He went to great lengths to explain about the man we've come to know as Doubting Thomas; he thought that was an incident in the life of Christ about the fact it was OK to question. And that Christ knew that Thomas needed to feel his wounds; feel the wounds in His side and feel the wounds in His hands. That it was what Thomas needed — he needed that physical contact. And then, of course, Christ said when you can accept this on faith, it will be even better.

I [liked] the fact that my father didn't brush aside my questions about faith. He allowed me as someone who lives in my mind to also live in my faith.

In this job, when we faced a horrible crisis like September 11, you go back in your mind and think, 'Is there anything I could have done? Might I have seen this coming? Was there some way?'

When you go through something like that, you have to turn to faith because you can rationalize it, you can make an intellectual answer about it but you can't fully accept it until you can feel it here [taps chest]. That time wasn't a failure, but it was a period of crisis when faith was really important for me.

I try always not to think that I am Elijah, that I have somehow been particularly called like a prophet. That's a dangerous thing. In a sense, we've all been called to whatever it is we are doing. But if you try to wear the imprimatur of God – I've seen that happen to leaders who begin too much to believe in that – then there are a couple of very good antidotes to that. I try to say when I pray, 'Help me to walk in Your way, not my own.' To try to walk in a way that is actually fulfilling a plan, and recognize you are a cog in a larger universe.

I think people who believe in the Creator can never take themselves too seriously. I feel that faith allows me to have a kind of optimism about the future. You look around you and you see an awful lot of pain, suffering and things that are going wrong. It could be oppressive. But when I look at my own story or many others that I have seen, I think, 'How could it possibly be that it has turned out this way?' Then my only answer is it's God's plan. And that makes me very optimistic that this is all working out in a proper way. So we must all stay close to God and pray and follow in His footsteps.

I really do believe that God will never let his children fall too far. There is an old gospel hymn, 'He knows how much you can bear.' I really do believe that. I greatly appreciate, and so does the President, the prayers of the American people. You feel them. You know that they are there. If you just keep praying for us, it is so important to all of us.

In many ways, it's a wonderful White House to be in because there are a lot of people who are of faith, starting with the President. When you are in a community of the faithful, it makes a very big difference not only in how people treat each other but in how they treat the task at hand.

Among American leadership, there are an awful lot of people who travel in faith. It's a remarkable thing and I think it probably sets us apart from most developed countries where it is not something that is appreciated quite as much in most of the world.

I've watched over the last year and a half how people want to have human dignity worldwide. You hear of Asian values or Middle Eastern values and how that means people can't really take to democracy or they'll never have democracy because they have no history of it, and so forth. We forget that when people are given a choice between freedom and tyranny, they will choose freedom. I remember all the stories before the liberation of Afghanistan that that nation wouldn't 'get it,' that they were all warlords and it would just be chaos. Then we got pictures of people dancing on the streets of Kabul just because they now could listen to music or send their girls to school.

(*The Layman*, October 2002, www.layman.org)

War Without Rules[1]

George Monbiot

George Monbiot is the author of the best-selling books *The Age of Consent: a manifesto for a new world order* and *Captive State: the corporate takeover of Britain*; as well as the investigative travel books *Poisoned Arrows*, *Amazon Watershed* and *No Man's Land*. He writes a weekly column for the *Guardian* newspaper.

Did US troops use chemical weapons in Fallujah? The answer is yes. The proof is not to be found in the documentary broadcast on Italian TV last week, which has generated gigabytes of hype on the Internet. It's a turkey, whose evidence that white phosphorus was fired at Iraqi troops is flimsy and circumstantial. But the bloggers debating it found the smoking gun.

The first account they unearthed comes from a magazine published by the US Army. In the March 2005 edition of *Field Artillery*, officers from the 2nd Infantry's Fire Support Element boast about their role in the attack on Fallujah in November last year. On page 26 is the following text. 'White Phosphorous. WP proved to be an effective and versatile munition. We used it for screening missions at two breeches and, later in the fight, as a potent psychological weapon against the insurgents in trench lines and spider holes when we could not get effects on them with HE [high explosives]. We fired "shake and

---

1   This article was first published in the *Guardian* on 15 November 2005.

bake" missions at the insurgents, using WP to flush them out and HE to take them out.'[2]

The second comes from a report in California's *North County Times*, by a staff reporter embedded with the Marines during the siege of Fallujah in April 2004. "'Gun up!" Millikin yelled ..., grabbing a white phosphorus round from a nearby ammo can and holding it over the tube. "Fire!" Bogert yelled, as Millikin dropped it. The boom kicked dust around the pit as they ran through the drill again and again, sending a mixture of burning white phosphorus and high explosives they call "shake 'n' bake" into a cluster of buildings where insurgents have been spotted all week.'[3]

White phosphorus is not listed in the schedules of the Chemical Weapons Convention. It can be legally used as a flare to illuminate the battlefield, or to produce smoke to hide troop movements from the enemy. Like other unlisted substances, it may be deployed for 'Military purposes ... not dependent on the use of the toxic properties of chemicals as a method of warfare'.[4] But it becomes a chemical weapon as soon as it is used directly against people. A chemical weapon can be 'any chemical which through its chemical action on life processes can cause death, temporary incapacitation or permanent harm'.

---

2 Captain James T. Cobb, First Lieutenant Christopher A. LaCour and Sergeant First Class William H. Hight, March 2005. 'TF 2-2 in FSE AAR: Indirect Fires in the Battle of Fallujah'. *Field Artillery*, March-April 2005.

3 Darrin Mortenson, 10 April 2004. 'Violence subsides for Marines in Fallujah.' *North County Times*. www.nctimes.com/articles/2004/04/11/military/iraq/19_30_504_10_04.txt

4 Article 2.9©. Convention on the Prohibition of the Development, Production, Stockpiling and Use of Chemical Weapons and on Their Destruction. The Organisation for the Prohibition of Chemical Weapons.

White phosphorus is fat-soluble and burns spontaneously on contact with the air. According to Globalsecurity.
org [a nonpartisan research group in Alexandria, Virginia],
'The burns usually are multiple, deep, and variable in size.
The solid in the eye produces severe injury. The particles
continue to burn unless deprived of atmospheric oxygen.
... If service members are hit by pieces of white phosphorus, it could burn right down to the bone.'[5] As it oxidizes,
it produces a smoke composed of phosphorous pentox-
ide. According to the standard US industrial safety sheet,
the smoke 'releases heat on contact with moisture and will
burn mucous surfaces. ... Contact with substance can cause
severe eye burns and permanent damage.'[6]

Until last week, the US State Department maintained
that US forces used white phosphorus shells 'very spar-
ingly in Fallujah, for illumination purposes. They were
fired into the air to illuminate enemy positions at night,
not at enemy fighters.'[7] Confronted with the new evidence,
on Thursday it changed its position. 'We have learned that
some of the information we were provided ... is incorrect.
White phosphorous shells, which produce smoke, were
used in Fallujah not for illumination but for screening
purposes, i.e., obscuring troop movements and, according
to ... *Field Artillery* magazine, "as a potent psychological
weapon against the insurgents in trench lines and spider
holes ..." The article states that US forces used white

5   www.globalsecurity.org/military/systems/munitions/wp.htm
6   Mallinckrodt Baker, Inc., 2 November 2001. Material Safety Data Sheet: Phos-
    phorus Pentoxide. http://164.107.52.42/MSDS/P phosphorous%20pentoxide.
    pdf
7   US State Department, viewed 9 November 2005. 'Did the US Use "Illegal"
    Weapons in Fallujah?' http://usinfo.state.gov/media/Archive_Index/Illegal_
    Weapons_in_Fallujah.html

phosphorous rounds to flush out enemy fighters so that
they could then be killed with high explosive rounds.'[8]
The US government, in other words, appears to admit
that white phosphorus was used in Fallujah as a chemical
weapon.

The invaders have been forced into a similar climbdown
over the use of napalm in Iraq. In December 2004, the
Labour MP Alice Mahon asked the British Armed Forces
Minister Adam Ingram 'whether napalm or a similar
substance has been used by the coalition in Iraq (a) during
and (b) since the war'. 'No napalm,' the minister replied,
'has been used by coalition forces in Iraq either during the
war-fighting phase or since.'[9]

This seemed odd to those who had been paying attention. There were widespread reports that in March 2003
US Marines had dropped incendiary bombs around the
bridges over the Tigris and the Saddam Canal on the way
to Baghdad. The commander of Marine Air Group 11
admitted that 'We napalmed both those approaches'.[10]
Embedded journalists reported that napalm was dropped
at Safwan Hill on the border with Kuwait.[11] In August
2003 the Pentagon confirmed that the Marines had

---

8   US State Department, viewed 14 November 2005. 'Did the US Use "Illegal"
    Weapons in Fallujah?' http://usinfo.state.gov/media/Archive_Index/Illegal_
    Weapons_in_Fallujah.html. The change was brought to my attention by The
    Cat's Dream: www.thecatsdream.com/blog/2005/11/exclusive-us-depart-
    ment-of_113178537408786105.htm
9   Adam Ingram, 6 December 2004. Written answer. Hansard Column
    339W, 201991. www.publications.parliament.uk/pa/cm200405/cmhansrd/
    cm041206/text/41206w19.htm
10 Colonel Randolph Alles, quoted by James W. Crawley, 5 August 2003. 'Offi-
    cials confirm dropping firebombs on Iraqi troops.' San Diego Union-Tribune.
    www.signonsandiego.com/news/military/20030805-9999_1n5bomb.html
11 For example, Martin Savidge, 22 March 2003. 'Protecting Iraq's oil supply.'
    CNN. http://edition.cnn.com/2003/WORLD/meast/03/21/otsc.irq.savidge/

dropped 'Mark 77 firebombs.' Though the substance they contained was not napalm, its function, the Pentagon's information sheet said, was 'remarkably similar'.[12] While napalm is made from petrol and polystyrene, the gel in the Mark 77 is made from kerosene and polystyrene. I doubt it makes much difference to the people it lands on.

So in January this year, the MP Harry Cohen refined Alice Mahon's question. He asked 'whether Mark 77 firebombs have been used by Coalition forces'. 'The United States,' the minister replied 'have confirmed to us that they have not used Mark 77 firebombs, which are essentially napalm canisters, in Iraq at any time.'[13] The US government had lied to him. Mr Ingram had to retract his statements in a private letter to MPs in June.[14]

We were told that the war with Iraq was necessary for two reasons. Saddam Hussein possessed biological and chemical weapons and might one day use them against another nation. And the Iraqi people needed to be liberated from his oppressive regime, which had, among its other crimes, used chemical weapons to kill them. Tony Blair, Colin Powell, William Shawcross, David Aaronovitch, Nick Cohen, Ann Clwyd and many others referred, in making their case, to Saddam's gassing of the Kurds in Halabja in 1988. They accused those who opposed the war of caring nothing for the welfare of the Iraqis.

12 James W. Crawley, 5 August 2003. 'Officials confirm dropping firebombs on Iraqi troops.' *San Diego Union-Tribune*. www.signonsandiego.com/news/military/20030805-9999_1n5bomb.html

13 Adam Ingram, 11 January 2005. Written answer. Hansard Column 374W, 207246. www.publications.parliament.uk/pa/cm200405/cmhansrd/cm050111/text/50111w01.htm#50111w01.html_sbhd3

14 Colin Brown, 17 June 2005. 'US lied to Britain over use of napalm in Iraq war.' The *Independent*.

Given that they care so much, why has none of these hawks spoken out against the use of unconventional weapons by coalition forces? Ann Clwyd, the Labour MP who turned from peace campaigner to chief apologist for an illegal war, is, as far as I can discover, the only one of these armchair warriors to engage with the issue. In May this year, she wrote to the *Guardian* to assure us that reports that a 'modern form of napalm' has been used by US forces 'are completely without foundation. Coalition forces have not used napalm – either during operations in Fallujah, or at any other time.'[15] How did she know? The Foreign Office Minister told her. Before the invasion, Ann Clwyd travelled through Iraq to investigate Saddam's crimes against his people. She told the Commons that what she had discovered moved her to tears. After the invasion, she took the minister's word at face value, when a thirty-second search on the Internet could have told her it was bunkum. It makes you wonder whether she, or any of the other enthusiasts for war, really gave a damn about the people for whom they claimed to be campaigning.

Saddam Hussein, facing a possible death sentence, is accused of mass murder, torture, false imprisonment, the embezzlement of billions and the use of chemical weapons. He is certainly guilty on all counts. So, it now seems, are the people who overthrew him.

---

15 Ann Clwyd, 2 May 2005. Letter to the *Guardian*.

The Siege of Fallujah and the Geneva Conventions

Jonathan Holmes

The siege of Fallujah, carried out by US armed forces upon a mainly civilian population, contravened seventy individual articles of the Geneva Conventions.[1]

The US, an original signatory to the Conventions, is in its activities in Iraq currently in breach of nearly every major area of concern identified by them. So careless is the US military of the Conventions that it is difficult to see how it could continue to function were it to adhere to them. Those in command have chosen to drive a tank through a century and a half of delicately crafted regulations on the treatment of those involved in conflict.

The Geneva Convention is in fact four conventions. Conventions One, Three and Four deal with the protection of the sick and wounded, of civilians, and of prisoners of war respectively (Convention Two deals with war at sea, and obviously does not apply here). The core of each of these has

---

1 At a conservative estimate, the specific articles ignored or violated by the US military in Fallujah are as follows: in Convention One (1949), articles 3, 4, 7, 12, 13, 15, 18, 19, 22, 24, 26, 30, 45, 46, annex articles 11 and 13. In Convention Four (1949), articles 2, 3, 4, 5, 8, 9, 10, 12, 16, 17, 18, 19, 20, 21, 23, 24, 27, 30, 33, 45, 55, 56, 59, 147, 148, 149, annex articles 11 and 12. In Added Protocol I (1977) articles 11, 14, 15, 20, 34, 35, 37, 40, 41, 53, 59, 77, 90, 91. In Added Protocol II (1977) articles 1, 5, 6, 7, 8, 9, 11, 13, 14, 15, 16, 17, 18. The Conventions are repetitive, meaning some of these articles cover the same areas of concern, but in general I have not included articles that directly duplicate one another – hence the omission of the Convention Three in this tally.

been gutted by American actions in Fallujah. The Conventions are the basis of international law in times of war, and are not a simply formality or series of guidelines; the American actions in Fallujah are therefore grave indeed.[2]

The US is not alone in violating the Conventions: the actions of so-called insurgents[3] and home-grown Iraqi rebel groups frequently do so as well. This article focuses on American actions for the following reasons. 1) The US is explicitly present in Iraq as liberator and guarantor of rights of the inhabitants. 2) Iraqi actions are made public every day, and legal recourse exists if and when the violators are apprehended. This is not the case for the US. 3) The US is present in a foreign sovereign state. Its actions are

---

2 The Geneva Conventions consist of four treaties formulated in Geneva, Switzerland, that set the standards for international law for humanitarian concerns. As per Articles 49, 50, 129 and 146 of the Geneva Conventions One, Two, Three and Four, respectively, all signatory states are required to enact sufficient national law to make grave violations of the Geneva Conventions a punishable criminal offence.

The conventions and their agreements are as follows: Convention One *'for the Amelioration of the Condition of the Wounded and Sick in Armed Forces in the Field'* (1949). Convention Two *'for the Amelioration of the Condition of Wounded, Sick and Shipwrecked Members of Armed Forces at Sea'* (1949). Convention Three *'relative to the Treatment of Prisoners of War'* (1949). Convention Four *'relative to the Protection of Civilian Persons in Time of War'* (1949). In addition, there are three additional protocols to the Geneva Convention:

Protocol I (1977): Protocol Additional to the Geneva Conventions of 12 August 1949, and relating to the Protection of Victims of International Armed Conflicts. Protocol II (1977): Protocol Additional to the Geneva Conventions of 12 August 1949, and relating to the Protection of Victims of Non-International Armed Conflicts. Protocol III (2005): Protocol Additional to the Geneva Conventions of 12 August 1949, and relating to the Adoption of an Additional Distinctive Emblem

3 'Insurgent' is a textbook example of doublespeak; the people referred to by the term are generally civilians, sometimes involved in a piecemeal resistance movement with guerrilla factions. Occasionally they are what would elsewhere be referred to as terrorists.

therefore of more than usual concern. Finally, it is almost impossible for Fallujan citizens to inform the world at large of their predicament, whereas the Americans control many media outlets and channels of information.

Of course, the US is not alone in committing atrocities in Iraq – the British must also shoulder some of this burden, though to a markedly lesser extent, for their actions in Basra and elsewhere in the south of the country, as must those in charge of the tens of thousands of mercenary soldiers currently fighting for the highest bidder. But Fallujah is the subject of this book, and, though supplemented by mercenaries, the forces besieging and occupying that city were and are from the US.

The sick and wounded

In Convention One (C1), it is expressly stated that all wounded personnel be given full medical treatment at the earliest opportunity without prejudice. US snipers have openly discussed acting in direct contradiction of this principle:

> Sometimes a guy will go down, and I'll let him scream a bit to destroy the morale of his buddies... then I'll use a second shot.[4]

This contravenes Article 1, the founding principle of each of the Conventions, and only too neatly encapsulates the US attitude to the conflict in the city. The American tactic of so-called 'double-tapping', in which wounded individuals were dispatched by two point-blank gunshots to the head, obviously and horrifically contravenes every aspect

---

4   Quoted by Tony Perry, *Los Angeles Times*. 17 April 2004.

of the articles concerning protection of the sick. A series of interviews by Bob Graham of the *London Evening Standard* with US personnel confirms this:

> Such is their level of hatred they [US troops] preferred to kill rather than merely injure. Sergeant Meadows, 34, said: 'The worst thing is to shoot one of them, then go help him.' Sergeant Adrian Pedro Quinones, 26, chipped in: 'In that situation you're angry, you're raging. They'd just been shooting at my men – they were putting my guys in a casket and eight feet under, that's what they were trying to do. And now, they're laying there and I have to help them, I have a responsibility to ensure my men help them [?].' Corporal Richardson said: 'Shit, I didn't help any of them. I wouldn't help the fuckers. There were some you let die. And there were some you double-tapped.' He held out his hand as if firing a gun and clucked his tongue twice. He said: 'Once you'd reached the objective, and once you'd shot them and you're moving through, anything there, you shoot again. You didn't want any prisoners of war. You hate them so bad while you're fighting, and you're so terrified, you can't really convey the feeling, but you don't want them to live.'[5]

In a separate incident, the BBC reported on a video of double-tapping made available at the end of 2004 (and now freely available on the Internet):

> The US military has announced it is looking into whether an American marine in Fallujah shot dead a severely wounded Iraqi insurgent at point-blank range. Television footage shows US soldiers entering a building as injured prisoners lie on the floor. The soldier, who has not been

---

5   Bob Graham, 'I Just Pulled the Trigger', *London Evening Standard,* 20 June 2003.

identified, has been removed from the field and faces possible charges. Lieutenant General John Sattler promised to pursue the facts of the case 'thoroughly' before taking further measures.

US-led forces said they have now gained overall control in Fallujah, trapping rebels in the south of the city. The images of the alleged point-blank shooting of an Iraqi insurgent were taken by an NBC reporter embedded with the US troops in the Sunni city under assault.

They show a group of Marines from the 3rd Battalion, 1st Regiment, armed with rifles, entering a building near a mosque last Saturday, 13 November. The mosque had been used by insurgents to attack US forces, who had stormed it a day earlier, killing ten militants and wounding five.

At least three severely wounded men are seen in a room inside the building – two are slumped against one of the walls, partially covered with a blanket. The NBC's Kevin Sites says the wounded men had been left in the mosque after being treated by a group of Marines following Friday's fighting. Mr Sites says soldiers from a different unit went and apparently shot the men again on Saturday without knowing whether they were armed. 'Then one of the Marines points his rifle at the head of one of the injured, an old man, saying, "He's faking he's dead",' Mr Sites' description continues. 'The sound of a shot is then heard. And in the background, another soldier says, "Well, he's dead now".'

Gen Sattler, commander of the 1st Marine Expeditionary Force, said the purpose of the investigation was to determine 'whether the Marine acted in self-defence, violated military law or failed to comply with the law of armed conflict'. 'We follow the law of armed conflict and we hold ourselves to a high standard of accountability.' Gen Sattler said.[6]

---

6   http://news.bbc.co.uk/1/hi/world/middle_east/4014901.stm\
Tuesday, 16 November, 2004, 13:37 GMT.

The accounts given by several Iraqi civilians, concerning the deliberate mutilation and killing of survivors and innocent family members in homes being searched, also very clearly runs counter to the Conventions. Article 3 of C1 states:

Art. 3. (...) each Party to the conflict shall be bound to apply, as a minimum, the following provisions:

(1) Persons taking no active part in the hostilities, including members of armed forces who have laid down their arms and those placed *hors de combat* by sickness, wounds, detention, or any other cause, shall in all circumstances be treated humanely, without any adverse distinction founded on race, colour, religion or faith, sex, birth or wealth, or any other similar criteria. To this end, the following acts are and shall remain prohibited at any time and in any place whatsoever with respect to the above-mentioned persons:

(a) violence to life and person, in particular murder of all kinds, mutilation, cruel treatment and torture;

(b) taking of hostages;

(c) outrages upon personal dignity, in particular humiliating and degrading treatment;

(d) the passing of sentences and the carrying out of executions without previous judgement pronounced by a regularly constituted court, affording all the judicial guarantees which are recognized as indispensable by civilized peoples.

(2) The wounded and sick shall be collected and cared for. An impartial humanitarian body, such as the International Committee of the Red Cross, may offer its services to the Parties to the conflict. The Parties to the conflict should further endeavour to bring into force, by means of special agreements, all or part of the other provisions of the present Convention. The application of the preceding provisions shall not affect the legal status of the Parties to the conflict.

Bob Graham's interviews, cited above, again demonstrate just how far from honouring this article US military actions were:

> By their own admission these American soldiers have killed civilians without hesitation, shot wounded fighters and left others to die in agony.
>
> Sergeant First Class John Meadows revealed the mindset that has led to hundreds of innocent Iraqi civilians being killed alongside fighters deliberately dressed in civilian clothes. 'You can't distinguish between who's trying to kill you and who's not,' he said. 'Like, the only way to get through s*** like that was to concentrate on getting through it by killing as many people as you can, people you know are trying to kill you. Killing them first and getting home.'
>
> These GIs, from Bravo Company of the 3/15th US Infantry Division, are caught in an impossible situation. Their attitude to these dangers is summed up by Specialist (Corporal) Michael Richardson, 22. 'There was no dilemma when it came to shooting people who were not in uniform, I just pulled the trigger. It was up close and personal the whole time, there wasn't a big distance. If they were there, they were enemy, whether in uniform or not. Some were, some weren't.'
>
> Specialist Anthony Castillo added: 'When there were civilians there we did the mission that had to be done. When they were there, they were at the wrong spot, so they were considered enemy.' In one major battle – at the southern end of Baghdad at the intersection of the main highways – the soldiers estimate about 70 per cent of the enemy's 400-or-so fighters were dressed as civilians.
>
> Sergeant Meadows explained: 'The fight lasted for about eight hours and they just kept on coming all day from everywhere, from all sides. They were all in plain clothes. We had dropped fliers a couple of days prior saying to people to

get out of the area if they didn't want to fight, so basically anyone who was there was a combatant. If they were dumb enough to stand in front of tanks or drive a car towards a tank, then they were there to fight. On that day it took away the dilemma of who to fire at, anyone who was there was a combatant.' [7]

The denial by US forces of access by Red Cross and Red Crescent personnel also derogates Part II of this article, while Article 4 – which makes provision for collecting and attending to the dead – is ignored in the accounts of bodies being left by the roadside (several journalists testify to this) and being eaten by dogs. As Dahr Jamail reported in November 2004:

IPs, who are under US control, have looted Fallujah General Hospital. The military stopped the Red Crescent at the gates of the city and are not allowing them in. They allowed some bodies to be buried, but others are being eaten by dogs and cats in the streets, as reported by refugees just out of the city, as well as residents still trapped there.[8]

Article 18 permits the inhabitants of a war zone 'spontaneously to collect and care for wounded or sick of whatever nationality'. Jo Wilding's graphic account (see pages 36 to 37) of trying to reach a woman giving birth in a clearly marked ambulance makes it obvious that US troops showed no regard at all for the care of the wounded, or of expectant mothers, who are also given special provision in Article 26 of Convention Four.

---

7   Graham, *op. cit.*
8   www.dahrjamailiraq.com/weblog/archives/2004_11_14.php

Convention One also goes to great lengths to stipulate protection and independence for medical units and hospitals. Article 19 states:

> Fixed establishments and mobile medical units of the Medical Service may in no circumstances be attacked, but shall at all times be respected and protected by the Parties to the conflict.

This provision is supported and reiterated at length in Annexe 1 to Convention One, which summarizes with the statement, in Article 11, that:

> In no circumstances may hospital zones be the object of attack. They shall be protected and respected at all times by the Parties to the conflict.

Other sections of the Convention, and of Conventions Three and Four and their annexes, repeat and stress again the necessity of hospitals and medical units in general to be free from attack of any kind: it is one of the central tenets of the whole Convention. The assault upon medical facilities in Fallujah therefore constitutes one of the most significant violations, and is evidently a serious human rights abuse on a large scale. The following is a quotation from Dahr Jamail's reports cited earlier:

> One of my colleagues, Dr Saleh Alsawi, he was speaking so angrily about them. He was in the main hospital when they raided it at the beginning of the siege. They entered the theater room when they were working on a patient …he was there because he's an anaesthesiologist. They entered with their boots on, beat the doctors and took them out, leaving the patient on the table to die.[9]

---

9 *Ibid.*

Again, many eyewitnesses corroborate Jamail's reporting, and US reconnaissance photography clearly identi-
fies hospitals as targets. There is no evidence of a Fallujan
hospital being used as a site of resistance, nor of any arms
being found within one – though even if they had, Article 22
of Convention One permits hospital orderlies to be armed
and a medical site of any description to be patrolled by
armed personnel. Jo Wilding, whilst travelling in a clearly
marked ambulance, was repeatedly targeted by snipers,
which once again displays blatant disregard for the provisions of the Convention: in an additional Protocol agreed
in 1977 an entire section (Section II), comprising ten individual articles, is devoted to blanket protection of medical
transportation of all kinds.

In claiming – falsely – that Fallujah contained no civilians the US is attempting to justify its refusal to allow the
International Red Cross to enter. However, the specific
remit of the IRC includes attending to injured combatants
and prisoners, so once again the refusal displays not only
callous indifference to human life but also ignorance of the
Geneva Conventions – Article 24 states:

> Medical personnel exclusively engaged in the search for,
> or the collection, transport or treatment of the wounded
> or sick, or in the prevention of disease, staff exclusively
> engaged in the administration of medical units and estab-
> lishments, as well as chaplains attached to the armed forces,
> shall be respected and protected in all circumstances.

In summary, Convention One reiterates in Article 50 what
it considers 'grave' breaches of the treaty:

Grave breaches...shall be those involving any of the following acts, if committed against persons or property protected by the Convention: wilful killing, torture or inhuman treatment, including biological experiments, wilfully causing great suffering or serious injury to body or health, and extensive destruction and appropriation of property, not justified by military necessity and carried out unlawfully and wantonly.

It is cruelly obvious, reading the accounts of Jo Wilding and Dahr Jamail, and the instructions of the US military themselves, that the Conventions have been wilfully disregarded and their principles trodden upon, and not only in the case of hospitals; innocent civilians too have been deliberately targeted.

Civilians

In a public announcement during April 2004, Brigadier-General Mark Kimmitt proclaimed:

Collective punishment is imposed on the people of Fallujah by those terrorists and cowards that hunker down inside mosques, hospitals and schools and use women and children as shields to hide.[10]

Article 33 of Convention Four (C4) states:

No protected person may be punished for an offence he or she has not personally committed. Collective penalties and likewise all measures of intimidation or of terrorism are

---

10   www.cpa-iraq.org/transcripts/20040401_Apr1_KimmittSenor.html: Briefing with Brigadier-General Kimmitt, Baghdad, 9.05am, 1 April , 2004.

prohibited. Pillage is prohibited. Reprisals against protected persons and their property are prohibited.

No evidence has ever been submitted demonstrating that hospitals or schools in the city were ever in the possession of insurgents; indeed, the only recorded instance of their takeover by military forces is when US troops occupied a school and ran amok through a hospital.

Included in this section of the protocol added in 1977 is a series of articles prohibiting perfidy, which is defined as: 'Acts inviting the confidence of an adversary to lead him to believe that he is entitled to, or is obliged to accord, protection under the rules of international law applicable in armed conflict, with intent to betray that confidence'. First among such acts is 'feigning to negotiate under a flag of truce'. Several witnesses report the following account, in this instance provided by Dr Salam Ismael.

The Iraqi National Guard used loudspeakers to call on people to get out of the houses carrying white flags, bringing all their belongings with them. They were ordered to gather outside near the Jamah al-Furkan mosque in the centre of town. On 12 November Eyad Naji Latif and eight members of his family – one of them a six-month old child – gathered their belongings and walked in single file, as instructed, to the mosque.

When they reached the main road outside the mosque they heard a shout, but they could not understand what was being shouted. Eyad told me it could have been 'now' in English. Then the firing began. US soldiers appeared on the roofs of surrounding houses and opened fire. Eyad's father was shot in the heart and his mother in the chest.

They died instantly. Two of Eyad's brothers were also hit, one in the chest and one in the neck. Two of the women were hit, one in the hand and one in the leg. Then the snipers killed the wife of one of Eyad's brothers. When she fell her five-year-old son ran to her and stood over her body. They shot him dead too. Survivors made desperate appeals to the troops to stop firing. But Eyad told me that whenever one of them tried to raise a white flag they were shot. After several hours he tried to raise his arm with the flag. But they shot him in the arm. Finally he tried to raise his hand. So they shot him in the hand. The five survivors, including the six-month-old child, lay in the street for seven hours. Then four of them crawled to the nearest home to find shelter.

The next morning the brother who was shot in the neck also managed to crawl to safety. They all stayed in the house for eight days, surviving on roots and one cup of water, which they saved for the baby. On the eighth day they were discovered by some members of the Iraqi National Guard and taken to hospital in Fallujah. They heard the Americans were arresting any young men, so the family fled the hospital and finally obtained treatment in a nearby town.

They do not know in detail what happened to the other families who had gone to the mosque as instructed. But they told me the street was awash with blood.

Our small convoy of trucks and vans brought 15 tons of flour, eight tons of rice, medical aid and 900 pieces of clothing for the orphans. We knew that thousands of refugees were camped in terrible conditions in four camps on the outskirts of town. There we heard the accounts of families killed in their houses, of wounded people dragged into the streets and run over by tanks, of a container with the bodies of 481 civilians inside, of premeditated murder, looting and acts of savagery and cruelty that beggar belief.[11]

The deliberate targeting and killing of civilians, in this instance carrying white flags, is indeed perfidious. Moreover, it is forbidden by the above protocol not to offer quarter either to civilians or to those placed *hors de combat*. It is clear that quarter was rarely given in Fallujah, whether to the wounded, the surrendered, the innocent or the civilian. Testimony and video records confirm this. The American explanation that the civilian population concealed 'insurgents' also is invalid, as Article 50 of the 1977 Protocol reads:

> The presence within the civilian population of individuals who do not come within the definition of civilians does not deprive the population of its civilian character.

Therefore the civilian population 'shall not be the object of attack or of reprisals', and in the case of structures devoted to civilian purposes, such as schools and places of worship, these places should remain protected. A senior British commander has gone on record to illustrate just how distant the US actions have been from the accepted rule of law:

---

11 Dr Ismael's account, dated 19 February 2005, differs slightly from the interview he gave anonymously to Dahr Jamial on 8 February. There are two variations: the age of the dead child and the number of people initially assembling at the meeting point. It is impossible to verify the reasons behind these differences but readers can compare Dahr Jamial's account with the accounts on http://hannah.webserver.smith-family.com:8080/archive/000929.html and www.socialistworker.co.uk/article.php4?article_id=5892.

Senior British commanders have condemned American military tactics in Iraq as heavy-handed and disproportionate. One senior Army officer told The *Telegraph* that America's aggressive methods were causing friction among allied commanders and that there was a growing sense of 'unease and frustration' among the British high command.

The officer, who agreed to the interview on the condition of anonymity, said that part of the problem was that American troops viewed Iraqis as *untermenschen* – the Nazi expression for 'sub-humans'. Speaking from his base in southern Iraq, the officer said: 'My view and the view of the British chain of command is that the Americans' use of violence is not proportionate and is over-responsive to the threat they are facing. They don't see the Iraqi people the way we see them. They view them as *untermenschen*. They are not concerned about the Iraqi loss of life in the way the British are. Their attitude towards the Iraqis is tragic, it's awful.

'The US troops view things in very simplistic terms. It seems hard for them to reconcile subtleties between who supports what and who doesn't in Iraq. It's easier for their soldiers to group all Iraqis as the bad guys. As far as they are concerned Iraq is bandit country and everybody is out to kill them.'

The phrase *untermenschen* – literally 'under-people' – was brought to prominence by Adolf Hitler in his book *Mein Kampf*, published in 1925. He used the term to describe those he regarded as racially inferior: Jews, Slavs and gypsies.

The officer explained that, under British military rules of war, British troops would never be given clearance to carry out attacks similar to those being conducted by the US military, in which helicopter gunships have been used to fire on targets in urban areas. British rules of engagement only allow troops to open fire when attacked, using the minimum force necessary and only at identified targets. The American approach was markedly different: 'When US troops are attacked with mortars in Baghdad, they use mortar-locating radar to find the firing point and then attack the general area with artillery, even though the area they are attacking may be in the middle of a densely populated residential area.

'They may well kill the terrorists in the barrage but they will also kill and maim innocent civilians. That has been their response on a number of occasions. It is trite, but American troops do shoot first and ask questions later. They are very concerned about taking casualties and have even trained their guns on British troops, which has led to some confrontations between soldiers.' The British response in Iraq has been much softer. During and after the war the British set about trying to win the confidence of the local population. There have been problems, it hasn't been easy but on the whole it was succeeding. 'The US will have to abandon the sledgehammer-to-crack-a-nut approach – it has failed,' he said. 'They need to stop viewing every Iraqi, every Arab as the enemy and attempt to win the hearts and minds of the people.'[12]

The views expressed in this article echo my own experiences interviewing senior British officers stationed in Iraq. The following are the views of a senior-ranking officer who cannot be named:

The solution to law and order is simple – we did it in Northern Ireland – joint patrols with the Iraqi police. People don't mind the guilty being searched. Unfortunately, we disbanded the Iraqi police a year ago. You have to remember, the Pentagon is run by guys who fought in Vietnam.

12 Sean Rayment, *Daily Telegraph*, 11 April 2004.

Their instinctive response is still 'take 'em out in a major combat operation'. The Americans are at war, the British are fighting a counter-insurgency operation. Plus, of course, there is little or no appetite in the Pentagon or in the White House for substantial change. They go in with immediate victory in mind, not effectual change.[13]

Of course, it should once again be recalled that the UK is not blameless in its behaviour in Iraq, especially at a policy level. There have been courts martial in response to abuse of prisoners and civilians, and many other allegations of a disturbing nature. Nevertheless, the command structure and intelligence processes in operation in the British Army make it significantly more flexible, adaptable and responsible as an entity than the US military. The distinction made by my source at the end of the above quotation is also significant: the American military mindset is one of winning or losing, and therefore unsuited to a confused and complex situation such as Iraq, whereas the British are only too used to coping with transition and post-colonial fragmentation – a grimly ironic byproduct of the United Kingdom's imperialist past.

The US attitude is made especially bewildering given the quality of the weapons systems available to them: they are able to pinpoint targets accurately, yet they still choose to wipe out entire communities, whether they are targets in themselves or not. Article 59 of the 1977 Protocol II provides for the protection on 'non-defended localities', which should not be subject of military attack. Each time

---

13 Interview conducted under the Chatham House Rule ('When a meeting, or part thereof, is held under the Chatham House Rule, participants are free to use the information received, but neither the identity nor the affiliation of the speaker(s), nor that of any other participant, may be revealed'), July 2005.

the US storms a house or bombs a street, it violates this article. The same Protocol, in Article 14, reaffirms the rights of civilians:

> Starvation of civilians as a method of combat is prohibited. It is therefore prohibited to attack, destroy, remove or render useless for that purpose, objects indispensable to the survival of the civilian population such as food-stuffs, agricultural areas for the production of food-stuffs, crops, livestock, drinking water installations and supplies and irrigation works.

The targeting of Fallujan resources nakedly derogates this article, and also Article 17, which asserts that 'Civilians shall not be compelled to leave their own territory for reasons connected with the conflict.' Dahr Jamail graphically illustrates how these guarantees have been violated:

> Fallujah … is 70 per cent bombed to the ground, no water, no electricity. People who want to go back into that city have to get retina scans, all ten fingers fingerprinted, then they're issued an ID card. People inside the city are referring to it as a big jail. It is a horrendous situation, and we still have hundreds of thousands of refugees as a result.[14]

We are used to such descriptions of cities from the Second World War, in which enemy armies fought each other, but in the current situation, in which a country is supposedly being liberated and its population considered allies, it is both disturbing and disgraceful.

---

14 www.democracynow.org/article.pl?sid=05/04/28/1346252

Illegal Weapons Use

The reason given for invading Iraq in the first place was, infamously, that the governing regime possessed weapons of mass destruction. These claims have since proved false, and it is likely that they were never believed to be true by the high command of either the UK or the USA in the first place. To compound this crime, the US forces, in 'liberating' Fallujah, have made extensive use of chemical weapons prohibited by international treaty, and which they themselves later claimed not to have used. In short, the US has invaded a nation on the pretext of disarming a non-existent arsenal, and in the process used its own weapons of mass destruction on the innocent civilian population it was supposed to be liberating. The hypocrisy and viciousness of this are staggering.

In its assault on Fallujah, the US military used both white phosphorus and napalm. In addition to the UN Charter, such weaponry is prohibited in the Geneva Convention added Protocol, Section III, Part III:

Article 35. Basic rules 1. In any armed conflict, the right of the Parties to the conflict to choose methods or means of warfare is not unlimited. 2. It is prohibited to employ weapons, projectiles and material and methods of warfare of a nature to cause superfluous injury or unnecessary suffering. 3. It is prohibited to employ methods or means of warfare which are intended, or may be expected, to cause widespread, long-term and severe damage to the natural environment.

Article 36. New weapons. In the study, development, acquisition or adoption of a new weapon, means or method of warfare, a High Contracting Party is under an obligation to determine whether its employment would, in some or all circumstances, be prohibited by this Protocol or by any other rule of international law applicable to the High Contracting Party.

American officers have themselves admitted to the use of napalm:

Marine Corps fighter pilots and commanders who have returned from the war zone have confirmed dropping dozens of incendiary bombs near bridges over the Saddam Canal and the Tigris River. The explosions created massive fireballs.

'We napalmed both those [bridge] approaches,' said Colonel Randolph Alles in a recent interview. He commanded Marine Air Group 11, based at Miramar Marine Corps Air Station, during the war. 'Unfortunately, there were people there because you could see them in the [cockpit] video. They were Iraqi soldiers there. It's no great way to die,' he added.

How many Iraqis died, the military couldn't say. No accurate count has been made of Iraqi war casualties. The bombing campaign helped clear the path for the Marines' race to Baghdad. During the war, Pentagon spokesmen disputed reports that napalm was being used, saying the Pentagon's stockpile had been destroyed two years ago. Apparently the spokesmen were drawing a distinction between the terms 'firebomb' and 'napalm.' If reporters had asked about firebombs, officials said yesterday they would have confirmed their use. What the Marines dropped, the spokesmen said yesterday, were 'Mark 77 firebombs.' They acknowledged those are incendiary devices with a function 'remarkably similar' to napalm weapons. Rather than using gasoline and benzene as the fuel, the firebombs use kerosene-based jet fuel, which has a smaller concentration of benzene.

Hundreds of partially loaded Mark 77 firebombs were stored on pre-positioned ammunition ships overseas, Marine Corps officials said. Those ships were unloaded in Kuwait during the weeks preceding the war. 'You can call it something other than napalm, but it's napalm,' said John Pike, defense analyst with Globalsecurity.org, a nonpartisan research group in Alexandria, Va.

During a recent interview about the bombing campaign in Iraq, Marine Corps Major General Jim Amos confirmed aircraft dropped what he and other Marines continue to call napalm on Iraqi troops on several occasions. He commanded Marine jet and helicopter units involved in the Iraq war and leads the Miramar-based 3rd Marine Air Wing.

...

Military experts say incendiary bombs can be an effective weapon in certain situations. Firebombs are useful against dug-in troops and light vehicles, said GlobalSecurity's Pike. 'I used it routinely in Vietnam,' said retired Marine Lieutenant General Bernard Trainor, now a prominent defense analyst. 'I have no moral compunction against using it. It's just another weapon.' And, the distinctive fireball and smell have a psychological impact on troops, experts said. 'The generals love napalm,' said Alles, who has transferred to Washington. 'It has a big psychological effect.'[15]

Ben Cubby, another independent journalist, reports on the strategies used by the US army to veil the use of chemical weapons:

---

15 www.signonsandiego.com/news/military/20030805-9999_1n5bomb.html 'Results are "remarkably similar" to using napalm', by James W. Crawley, *San Diego Union-Tribune*, 5 August 2003.

The Pentagon no longer officially uses the brand-name 'Napalm', but a similar sticky, inflammable substance known as 'fuel-gel mixture', contained in weapons called Mark 77 firebombs, was dropped on Iraqi troops near the Iraq-Kuwait border at the start of the war. 'I can confirm that Mark 77 firebombs were used in that general area,' Colonel Mike Daily of the US Marine Corps said. Colonel Daily said that US stocks of Vietnam-era napalm had been phased out, but that the fuel-gel mixture in the Mark 77s had 'similar destructive characteristics. Many folks (out of habit) refer to the Mark 77 as "napalm" because its effect upon the target is remarkably similar,' he said.

The inflammable fuel in Mark 77 firebombs is thickened with slightly different chemicals, and is believed to contain oxidizers, which make it harder to extinguish than Napalm-B. Neither weapon technically contains napalm. The chemical mixture that became known as 'napalm' – a combination of naphthalene and palmitate – was used only in the earliest versions of the weapon.

Napalm was banned by United Nations convention in 1980, but the US never signed the agreement. Use of Mark 77 firebombs is considered legal by the US military. Ms Toni McNeal, a spokesperson for Rock Island Arsenal, in Illinois, said the facility is currently producing a further 500 Mark 77s for the US Marine Corps. She said she did not consider the Mark 77s to be napalm bombs. But Mark 77s are referred to as 'napalm' in some current US inventories and public affairs documents. A US Navy public affairs document dated 22/10/99 says that the US Navy no longer uses napalm but 'the US Marine Corps has a requirement and uses it at ranges at Yuma and Twenty-Nine Palms.' Twenty-Nine Palms, in California, is the home base of some of the Marine Corps units that took part in the attack on Safwan Hill in Iraq.

Captain Robert Crum, USMC, Public Affairs spokesman
for Twenty-Nine Palms, said: 'MK 77s are not routinely
used in training at 29 Palms. Yet it would be inappropri-
ate to say that they are never – or never would be – used in
training here.' [16]

In addition, independent filmmaker Peter Harling has now
discovered video evidence of the use and effect of such
weaponry on Fallujan residents.

There can be no clearer or more terrible indication of
the hypocrisy of the rhetoric of liberation and democracy employed by the US, nor of the phoney ration-
ale for the invasion, than this. One nation forcing its
beliefs, economy and political structure upon another by
burning sections of its population alive does not sound
like democracy.

Recourse

The various parts of the Geneva Conventions make little
provision for action in the face of systematic abuse. Article
90 stipulates the need, in such a case, for an 'International
Fact-Finding Commission consisting of fifteen members
of high moral standing and acknowledged impartiality'. It
also, in the subsequent article, states that 'A Party to the
conflict which violates the provisions of the Conventions
or of this Protocol shall, if the case demands, be liable

---

16 www.smh.com.au/articles/2003/08/08/1060145828249.html
   New, improved and more lethal: son of napalm, by Ben Cubby, 8 August
   2003.

to pay compensation. It shall be responsible for all acts committed by persons forming part of its armed forces'.

The US is a world power of sufficient authority such that it is unlikely that its actions shall ever be examined and brought to book in the manner of smaller nations: the standards applied to the often despicable actions of rebels and insurgents will probably never be applied to the American military. Though the Geneva Conventions clearly indicate that the US should pay reparation for its injurious actions, this will never happen; indeed, the Iraqi government is currently compelled to reimburse the US and the World Bank for restructuring loans. As ever, one rule exists for the powerful, and another for the weak. In consequence, the afflicted parties will continue to have little other recourse but to underhand violence. If the party that sets the rules promptly smashes them to pieces, as is the case of the US in respect of the Geneva Conventions, what hope can those following a different system realistically have of fair treatment, or even of a fair hearing?

Though few people have a clear idea of the content of the Geneva Conventions, or of the extent to which it has been violated by the US, it continues to be a threat to those seeking the unmitigated abuse of power. Right-wing political parties continue to advocate its abolition; such an advocacy was in fact part of the British Conservative Party's 2005 election manifesto, written by current Tory leader David Cameron. Michael Howard, the then leader, publicly announced his intention to scrap the Conventions should he be elected.[17]

---

17 See in particular his comments in the BBC Question Time 'Leaders' Special', screened on 28 April 2005.

The ethos of the Geneva Conventions is that the innocent, the weak, the defeated and the injured be afforded all the protection possible in times of conflict. The ethos of the US government is that the weak and innocent are a hindrance to the acquisition of power and, occasionally, an opportunity for the expansion of profit. Such conflicting ideologies cannot co-exist, and it must therefore be sadly only a matter of time before the Conventions, and the upright principles they espouse, become a quaint tradition of the past. Such a passing will be to all our costs.

FALLUJAH: THE PLAY

Introduction to the Play

Fallujah is a piece of documentary theatre. That is to say, all the characters are based on real people and use only the words of those people. The situations they find themselves in actually happened, in the way that they are depicted. I have edited testimonies for length but I have not augmented them, with the exception of occasional greetings at the start of a scene.

In comparison with prose, theatre cannot create a sense of pictorial realism with anything like the equivalent level of conviction. Theatre as compared to prose, cannot give the audience access to detailed description, cross-referenced sources and comprehensive evidence. It is not, on the surface, the medium most suited to a documentary enterprise. Indeed, every major decision one makes as a producer – from casting to design to lighting – distances the material still further from its source.

Crafting a testimony play is therefore a process of reconciling authenticity with theatricality. The process is of course flawed: as soon as you remove testimony from its human source and substitute an actor's voice, authenticity is compromised. It is limited further as soon as you juxtapose two comments, or two events, that were not absolutely sequential in life. Life rarely has closure, whereas drama usually does. All this is to say that theatre, more than most artforms, struggles to represent events in as realistic or objective a manner as a textbook or a documentary film (themselves not uncompromised in this arena); but that this should not be a subject for apology, as it is a different medium doing a different job, and would err in imitating others too closely.

In the case of verbatim theatre, the audience recognizes the testimony as being of a different mimetic order to the conventional product of playwriting, and instinctively adjusts its response accordingly. Spectatorship consequently takes place on two levels: the reception of the performance on the level of art, and that of the script on the level of immediate testimony. The 'witnessing' experience is thus richer and more complex than is customary, and also more personal. All narratives depicting actual occurrences are mediated by knowledge and experience. There is constantly the possibility of a clear ethical truthfulness through art that can be equal, if not more total, than the contingent empirical truths of factual reporting. This is not to suggest that the latter should be neglected, only that it is time for the former to be respected actively as more complete and forceful than tends to be admitted.

My own starting point in writing this play has therefore been that it is impossible to present a fully authentic picture of the situation in Fallujah. A theatre cannot be made to look like a besieged city, however gifted the designer, never mind smell like one or feel like one. Documentary realism is not possible in this case, and my feeling is that it would be disingenuous to attempt it. Consequently, my guide was not so much authenticity as authority, and a sense of ethical responsibility to the sources rather than a kind of photographic mimicry.

Every scene in the play comes from testimony, and in most cases is supported by at least two independent sources. Nothing is described or presented that was not directly witnessed. The text comes from accounts written by witnesses (presented in the section on testimonies), transcripts of interviews carried out by reputable journalists and myself; in the case of the former, I have used only material previously published and vetted by the editorial processes of dependable news bureaux. Many of the remaining citations were taken from the Iraq Body Count Website, administered by the Oxford Research Group.

There is one exception to this rule, found in the character of Sasha. Sasha is a composite figure, built from testimony given by different journalists, and from Jo Wilding's weblogs. She is also, in the early scenes, based on my own role in the interview processes. In the question-and-answer scenes in which she participates, all the answers are verbatim and taken from the source identified, but sometimes the questions have been amended to make the focus of the scene clearer. Similarly, two scenes (6 and 14) have been dramatized from Jo Wilding's accounts, as a theatrical alternative to presenting them as monologue, though as with the rest of the play every detail in them is faithful to Jo's meticulous report of the events.

A surprising portion of the material used in this play is already in the public domain. At a conservative estimate, I would say about 60 per cent of the text fits into this category, including much of the more shocking material. Everything that is presented in the script as a public statement – briefings by military personnel, speeches, televised interviews, and so on – comes from sources anyone can access, many of them on the Internet. All statements and comments by the US military, in any form, are already a matter of public record. The rest is material gathered

through my own documentation of testimony. In these
latter cases there were always witnesses present, except for
a very small quantity of material gathered through tele-
phone interviews.

This play differs from most other plays of the recent
verbatim boom, in the breadth of material sought and in
the theatricality of its presentation. I made the decision
to include in the production a near-constant soundscape,
designed by Nitin Sawhney, to encourage the audience to
empathize with the predicament of those trapped in Fallujah,
and to enhance the aural dimension of the performance.
Similarly, the play is designed to be staged in a fluid and
dynamic fashion, with performers and audience sharing
the same space and often the same light, and with little or
no 'fourth wall' type boundary. I chose to do so in order
to implicate the audience viscerally in the action; a specta-
tor is forced to decide whether she engages directly with
the actor speaking to her, or removes herself further from
the action. Thus, watching this play is intrinsically a
political act. Many verbatim plays use direct address and
monologues, yet retain the fourth wall, which seems to me
to be a contradictory convention worth dispensing with.

Finally, although the play is truthful and grounded in
several dozen carefully documented sources, it makes no
claim to objectivity (it is worth remarking here that, despite
the protestations of practitioners, it is doubtful whether
any play is ever really impartial). These things happened,
these people said what they did, and it is not incompatible
with the veracity of these things to condemn the perpe-
trators. Of course we need to understand how and why
atrocities happen, and do our collective utmost to work
to prevent their repetition, but it seems to me an evasion

of responsibility – even perhaps unethical – not to take a stand on the morality of the event.

The script printed here is the play as it was in early 2007, before the play had gone into rehearsal. Plays change significantly during the rehearsal period, so there could be differences between this and the version of the script as performed.

Fallujah

Jonathan Holmes

The Romans create a desolation and call it a peace.

Tacitus

Mountains mourn and rivers faint and fail.
There is no city nor cornfield nor orchard. All is rock
*   and sand,*
Jostling together in the void, suspended by inward fires.

William Blake

This is a testimony play. With the exception of some of the questions asked by the reporter and a few linking phrases, all the words spoken are authentic and taken from interviews carried out by the playwright, or from transcripts of interviews carried out by others and from first-hand accounts by the individuals concerned. Equally, all situations depicted are taken from record and all matters of fact have been corroborated by at least two independent sources. All characters are modelled on real people; the character of the reporter is in fact an amalgam of several individuals.

Staging

The audience should be allowed to move around in a central section of the space, with chairs available if they want to sit down. The action happens all around them and among them as appropriate; a kind of inverted in-the-round. Only the very first scene should be fixed as end-on, though the press briefings and lecture will probably encourage such a configuration, but if there is leakage, so be it. Equally, the briefings and lecture could occur on a different side of the space, so that the audience perspective is constantly shifting. The audience should feel very much involved in the action. The staging should be as sparse as possible, to allow fluid movement across the space and easy transition between the two dominant dramatic modes of the piece – documentary realism and direct address to the audience. The play begins naturalistically, but this fragments as the piece progresses. There are screens on each wall.

The piece should be accompanied by a sophisticated soundscape throughout. This should not be underscore, or mere naturalistic assistance, but an active player in the action. Much of what happens in the play does so aurally, and it is the function of the sound to give the audience both a clear and a subliminal sense of what it is to be in Fallujah at this time. Aural scenography is limitless in the theatre, whereas the visual is restricted. The sonic landscape should be exploited to the utmost, therefore, to ground the play in realism, but also in emotion and atmosphere.

Setting

The action of the play takes place mainly in the months of April and November 2004: the only exceptions are the first scene, which takes place in October 2001, and the last one, which takes place in 2005.

Fallujah is a city about the size of Edinburgh, roughly forty miles west of Baghdad. It has long had a reputation as a militant city, and is a centre for Sunni Islam. For many years it was known also as a stronghold of the Ba'athist regime.

Fallujah was the site of the bloodiest battles of the Iraq war and subsequent occupation. The struggle is ongoing, but has had three points of particular intensity: April 2003, as part of the general invasion; April 2004, in response to the killing of four US contractors on 31 March; and November 2004, when the city was besieged with the alleged aim of capturing or killing Abu Musab al-Zarqawi.

Characters

Sasha, a reporter
Rana, an Iraqi aid worker
Jo, a British witness
Ahrar, another Iraqi aid worker
An Iraqi doctor
Condoleezza Rice
Luce, a French journalist
A journalist working for Al-Jazeera
An Iraqi cameraman
A British major
A senior British cleric
A US General
The US Ambassador
A US Sniper
A US Commander
Several US soldiers
Fallujan civilians, medical staff, aides, journalists, businessmen, spokespeople.

Principal Collaborators in the Project

Crew

Direction	Jonathan Holmes
Design	Lucy and Jorge Orta
Music	Nitin Sawhney
Lighting Design	Paul J Need
Costume Design	Lucy Wilkinson
Audio-visual	Nick Price
Music Assistant	Peter Readman
Design Assistant	Ana Maria Pena
Production Manager	Ellen Mainwood
Company Manager	Alice Bray
Stage Manager	Joe Fairweather Hole

Ilium Productions Limited is an independent company devoted to the creation of meaningful ethical art through collaboration with artists of international standing in a variety of different media. Our intention is to comment truthfully and urgently on issues that matter with artistic dexterity and creative power.

Creative team

Lucy and Jorge Orta
British-born Lucy Orta is one of Europe's leading contemporary artists who draws upon design and architecture to create socially or politically responsive artworks. She has received critical acclaim for her solo exhibitions at the

Barbican Curve Gallery in London; the Venice Biennale; and the Boijmans Museum, Rotterdam in 2005.

Lucy's partner, Jorge Orta from Argentina, has developed a pioneering body called 'Light-works' employing large-scale projections to embellish world heritage sites. Jorge also represented Argentina at the Venice Biennale in 1995.

Now working together in partnership, the Anglo-Argentine couple employ a range of techniques from sculpture, object-making and couture, to painting, printing and light projections. Using a range of communication strategies such as performance, interventions and public events, the team investigate crucial issues of the world today. These include the community and the social link, dwelling and habitat, nomadism and mobility, sustainable development, ecology and recycling.

Lucy Orta has received numerous awards for innovation and her most recent academic acheivement is the Rootstein Hopkins Chair at London College of Fashion, for the University of the Arts London since 2002.

The Ortas' current work includes: 'OrtaWater' on exhibition at the Continua Gallery in Beijing and 'Antarctic Village', an ambitious installation of tent-bivouac sculptures in Antarctica which tours to the *Biennale al Fin del Mundo* (Biennale at the End of the World) on Fire Island, Spring 2007. For more information visit www.studio-orta.com.

Note on illustrations: the images reproduced in the script illustrate some of Lucy and Jorge Orta's *Fallujah* artworks.

Nitin Sawhney

Firmly established as a world-class producer, song-writer, DJ, multi-instrumentalist, orchestral composer, and cultural pioneer, Sawhney has released seven studio albums, each one garnering critical acclaim. *Beyond Skin* (1999), was nominated for the prestigious Technics Mercury Music Prize and won the coveted South Bank Show Award. *Prophesy* (2001) won him a MOBO Award as well as the BBC Radio 3 Music Award. Clubland saw a welcomed return by Sawhney in 2004 with the release of *All Mixed Up* – the definitive Nitin Sawhney remix collection and *FabricLive.15*. Sawhney's seventh studio album, *Philtre*, was released in May 2005 and he is currently writing his eighth album *London Under Sound*. He has sold out many of the world's most prestigious venues with his album tours.

Sawhney is also one of the world's leading scorers for film and television, and to date he has scored for over forty films. His music for Channel 4's *Second Generation* saw him nominated for the prestigious Ivor Novello Award for Film and TV Composition in 2004. Recent works include scores for Oscar-nominated director Mira Nair's adaptation of Jhumpa Lahiri's *The Namesake* (Fox Searchlight 2007), as well as *Natural World Symphony* for the BBC. He is currently producing music for Sony Playstation 3's *Heavenly Sword* (starring Andy Serkis), and will also score *The Fifth Beatle*, a major studio film currently in production.

He has gained much recognition within the Classical community. In 2006 he composed a symphony to accompany Franz Osten's silent film classic, *A Throw of Dice*, which premiered with the London Symphony Orchestra at the Barbican. He has also worked with the BBC Concert Orchestra (*Natural World Symphony*) and the Philharmonia Orchestra (*The Namesake*). In 2004, Sawhney was commissioned by the City of Birmingham Symphony Orchestra and the Britten Sinfonia to compose several works. Other past commissions include *Urban Prophecies* for the Proms in 2000, as well as *Neural Circuits* for the Britten Sinfonia, and leading British pianist Joanna MacGregor, in 2001. Sawhney will premiere new works during his performance at the 2007 Proms in the Royal Albert Hall.

Sawhney also produced the *Varekai* album for Cirque du Soleil, and has written original scores for contemporary dancer Akram Khan's *Kaash* and *Zero Degrees* projects. He has since been commissioned to score the forthcoming adaptation of *Mahabharata* by Olivier-Award winning writer Stephen Clark and Simon McBurney's *A Disappearing Number* for Complicité.

Harriet Walter

Since training at LAMDA, Harriet has worked extensively in theatre, television, film and radio. She started with groups such as Common Stock, Joint Stock, 7:84 and Paines Plough and then moved on to the Royal Court, the National Theatre and the Royal Shakespeare Company. At the RSC, she has most recently performed as Cleopatra in Gregory Doran's *Antony and Cleopatra* alongside Patrick Stewart; appeared in *The Hollow Crown*; performed as Beatrice in *Much Ado About Nothing* directed by Gregory Doran; and as Lady Macbeth opposite Antony Sher in

Gregory Doran's production of *Macbeth*. Previous RSC roles include Helena in Trevor Nunn's production of *All's Well that Ends Well*, Skinner in Howard Barker's *The Castle* (Olivier Best Actress Nomination). In 1990 she received an Olivier Award for *Twelfth Night*, *Three Sisters* and *A Question of Geography*. She is an Associate Artist of the Royal Shakespeare Company.

Other recent theatre work includes Elizabeth I in Schiller's *Mary Stuart* at the Donmar Warehouse for which she received an Olivier Award nomination and was a winner of the *Evening Standard* Best Actress Award; *Life x 3* (the N.T. Lyttelton theatre and the Old Vic) for which she was nominated Best Actress in the Olivier Awards and Simon Gray's *The Late Middle Classes* directed by Harold Pinter.

Her film credits include *Babel*, *Bright Young Things*, *Villa des Roses*, *Onegin*, *The Governess*, *Bedrooms and Hallways*, *Sense and Sensibility*, Louis Malle's *Milou en Mai* and most recently *Atonement* for Working Title. Harriet has twice won the Sony Radio Academy Award for Best Actress in 1988 and 1991. She has also published two books: *Other People's Shoes* (published first by Viking/Penguin, then re-issued by Nick Hern Books) and *Macbeth* in the Faber series, *Actors on Shakespeare*. She was appointed CBE in the New Year's Honours List, 2000 and was made an Honorary D.Litt. at Birmingham University.

PROLOGUE

SCENE 1: An interview for Al-Jazeera. Washington DC. October 2001.

A TV studio. The usual faffing as microphones are rigged and so on. As much as possible the stage should appear as though it is in fact a TV studio, and the audience is a studio audience. To this end the space can be in the process of being lit, and technicians can be getting things sorted even as the audience enters. Eventually, the INTERVIEWER and CONDOLEEZZA RICE enter and the interview begins. The full interview is also filmed and shown on a screen at the rear of the stage. The audience is encouraged to applaud as the interviewee enters.

INTERVIEWER: Dr Rice, we would like to thank you very much for this opportunity that you give to Al-Jazeera and to our audience in the Arab and Muslim world.

DR RICE: Thank you very much for the opportunity to be with you.

INTERVIEWER: Since we have a limited time, let me start first with the latest development; the military action beginning last week in Iraq. We see from polls and from demonstrations in the street that while some governments support the US, the public on the streets in the Arab and Muslim world do not. Do you think that there is a problem because the US only relies on the support of governments, regardless of what the people think?

DR RICE: We, of course, have very good relations with a
number of governments in the Middle East. But we care
very much also about the people of the Middle East, the
Arab populations. And the United States is a place to
which many Arabs have looked as a place — we have a
number of Arab immigrants in the United States. We think
that the United States is a place in which religious tolerance and a belief that all people should live together in
peace is a message that would resonate with populations
in the region.

INTERVIEWER: So is it a problem of perception, an
image of the US only, or is it policies that are perceived to
be double standards and we need to review the US policies
in the Middle East?

DR RICE: No, we believe that the policies that the United
States is pursuing are ones that are good for the Middle
East as a whole.

INTERVIEWER: You are personally perceived as one of
the people in the administration who wanted to enlarge the
war in terrorism to include Iraq. Correct me, please.

DR RICE: Iraq has been a problem not just for US policy,
but for policy in the region, as well. This is a country that
has threatened its neighbours, that has been harmful to its
own people. And we believe that our policies toward Iraq
simply are to protect the region and to protect Iraq's people
and neighbours.

Now, we understood when we came to power here in
Washington that we had a problem, for instance, on Iraqi
sanctions; that people believed, or that Saddam Hussein
was claiming that the sanctions that were in place were

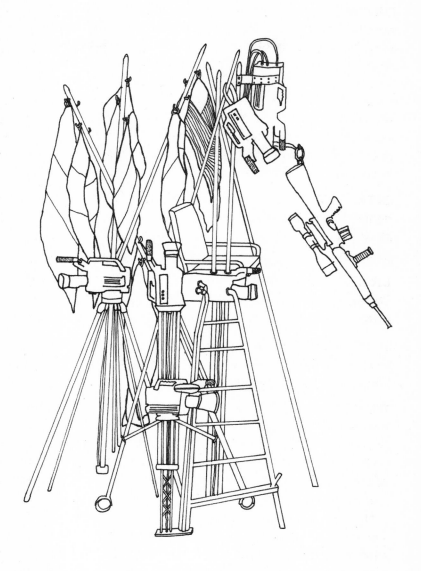

somehow harming the Iraqi people. We do not believe that they were harming the Iraqi people. But that said, we wanted to change the sanctions. We wanted to change the sanctions so that they are aimed at the regime, which is a danger to its neighbours, not at the people.

The President has made very clear that the war on terrorism is a broad war on terrorism. You can't be for terrorism in one part of the world and against it in another part of the world. We worry about Saddam Hussein. We worry about his weapons of mass destruction that he's trying to achieve.

INTERVIEWER: How about Syria?

DR RICE: We have had some discussions with Syria. The President, in his speech to the Joint Session, said: those who continue to harbour terrorists. That's an invitation to countries to stop the practice of harbouring terrorism.

INTERVIEWER: So if Syria does not cooperate against people who are from Jihad or Hamas or Hizbollah, they should be targeted also?

DR RICE: You can't say there are good terrorists and there are bad terrorists. But the means that we use with different countries to get them to stop harbouring terrorists may be very broad. And there are many means at our disposal. You cannot be neutral in this fight; you either are for terrorism or against it.

INTERVIEWER: Overall, how do you perceive Al-Jazeera as a credible or independent media?

DR RICE: Well, if I did not have respect for Al-Jazeera, I would not be doing this interview. The United States believes that the press is one of the most fundamental bases for democracy and for individuals to have the kind of dignity that human beings should have. And so I'm delighted to be here on Al-Jazeera. I know that you're going to have many of my colleagues on in the future, and I look forward to being back with you.

INTERVIEWER: Thank you. And I leave you at the end just with a statement from you without my interference, to our audience in the Arab and Muslim world, whatever you would like to tell them.

DR RICE: I would like to say to the Arab and Muslim world the following. I would like to say that America is a country that respects religious difference. America is a country that has many people of different religions within it. The fastest-growing religion in America is the Muslim faith.

This is a war against the evil of terrorism. The President of the United States understands Islam to be a faith of peace, a faith that protects innocents, and the policy of the United States is to do the same.

Thank you very much.

INTERVIEWER: Thank you, Dr Rice.

ACT ONE

SCENE 2: A press briefing. Baghdad, 3 April 2004.

As with the first scene, we are in a situation familiar to us from broadcast news – the press briefing with an anchorwoman present. Also as with the first scene, what we see is also screened. It is important that the camera angles and video quality accurately mimic those of, say, CNN. The date and location are displayed prominently on the screens. The AMBASSADOR is flanked by military top brass.

SASHA (*to camera*): Since the first assault on the city last year Fallujah has been at the sensitive heart of the US presence in Iraq. Violent and determined opposition to the occupation has been at its most intense in the city, and for six months coalition forces have been placed in an increasingly difficult position in the face of such committed resistance. The discovery of the burned, brutalized and mutilated bodies of four American civilian contractors, working for Blackwater Security, can only intensify the already volatile situation.

AMBASSADOR (*to assembled journalists*): The deaths of these four men outside Fallujah and their despicable mutilation will not derail the march toward stability and democracy in Iraq. The attacks will not go unpunished. The US will respond at the time and place of our choosing.

SASHA: Mr Ambassador, will this affect the June 30th handover?

AMBASSADOR: We have problems, there's no hiding that. But basically Iraq is on track to realize the kind of Iraq that Americans want – and that Iraqis want – which is a democratic Iraq. Thank you. (*He leaves.*)

SASHA: General, can you tell us a little of your plans in response to these murders? Do you know who is responsible?

US GENERAL: We are going to hunt down the people responsible for this bestial act. It will be at a time and a place of our choosing. We are not going to do a pell-mell rush into the city. It will be deliberate, it will be precise and it will be overwhelming. We will not rush in to make things worse. We will plan our way through this and we will re-establish control of that city and we will pacify that city. Good day.

SASHA: General, if I could…

US GENERAL: I'm afraid that's all for today. Thank you.

REPORTERS: General, General….

SCENE 3: RANA.

RANA and AHRAR should appear unobtrusively. In fact, they have been watching the previous scenes on television. At a suitable juncture RANA addresses us directly. There should be no acknowledgement of a fourth wall – she is talking to us.

RANA: My job is to go to these cities under siege, negotiate with the Americans, go inside and look for women and children and the wounded, and try to get them out of the city if they want, or find them somewhere safe inside the city if we can. I work with friends using their holy passports – British, American – to get through checkpoints.

The resistance started after the peaceful protest in May at the school. The Americans shot about twenty people in the protest. So this is how it started. Fallujah is not a city with a history of resistance. You've heard that Fallujah was fighting for Saddam but it isn't true – Fallujah was the centre of the anti-Saddam coup in the nineties. Fallujah did not resist to start with. People said 'we were thinking the Americans came to help'. I was thinking 'they come to destroy Iraq'.

AHRAR: Under Saddam we'd be paid visits but they'd at least wait for us to answer the door. Under the Americans the doors are just kicked in. And now what? Go and vote and risk being blown to pieces, or followed by insurgents and murdered for cooperating with the Americans? For what? To practice democracy? Are you joking?

All I can say is that Fallujah is like it was struck by a tsunami. There weren't many families in there after the siege, but they had absolutely nothing. The suffering was beyond what you can imagine. When the Americans finally let us in people were fighting just for a blanket.

America can go to the moon. America can make weapons capable of killing from a world away. But America cannot make and replace people.

RANA turns on a small television set. The following scene is 'broadcast' on it, and on large screens on the walls. At the other side of the room, SASHA enters and watches the same footage on a different TV, which should then allow her to segue into Scene 5. NB: the basic principle here is that everything seen on the screens or played through the sound system is seen and heard by at least some of the characters. They are props the actors interact with, as well as alternative methods of storytelling for the audience.

SCENE 4: ONSCREEN ONLY. Fallujah.

RANA (ONSCREEN): The strange thing is, during the last days of the siege some people doing some cleaning in the street, and I'm like what's that? And we see trucks removing soil and bringing water to clean the streets. And the soldiers are giving toys to the kids, the few children left. And we drove a bit further and I see the crew of CNN filming and this is the footage the Americans see back home! Soldiers cleaning the streets, giving toys to the kids!.

CUT TO:

US COLONEL (ONSCREEN): We napalmed those bridges. Unfortunately, there were people there. It's no great way to die. The generals love napalm, it has a big psychological effect.

SCENE 5: Baghdad. SASHA, a British MAJOR and a senior Christian CLERIC. Also British.

The two men pass without initially seeing the journalist; they should have entered while the scene on the screen is being played, leaving no gap at all between that and the start of this scene.

SASHA: Sir?

MAJOR: Jesus, Sasha, do you have to skulk around like that?

CLERIC: Good morning, I'm afraid I haven't had the pleasure?

MAJOR: Ah, Sasha Edmonton, the doyenne of investigative journalism. If there are skeletons or choirboys in your closet, uncover them she will. Sasha, this is the vicar of Baghdad.

SASHA: Do you have time for me to ask you a few questions?

MAJOR: OK, Sasha. Because it's you. But we can't stay long.

SASHA: Rumour has it you've just come from a meeting with al-Sadr? And with Bremer?

CLERIC: Good grief, is nothing secret any more? You're well informed.

SASHA: And?

MAJOR: Off the record?

SASHA: OK. Yes *(switches off the recorder)*. Fully Chatham House. Tell me about the situation in Fallujah, please. What's your intelligence?

MAJOR: If you want to know about Fallujah, think of Londonderry in the early seventies. OK, so military intelligence used to be about finding various large bits of metal – tanks, guns, planes etc. We realized in Northern Ireland that actually it was about learning about hearts and minds. It's a change from hardware to software, if you like. In Iraq, we know where all the lumps of metal are, but not how the regime actually works. You have to remember that opening dialogue and other equivalent talking cures are not military processes, they're governmental and political processes. Whereas, if we pitch up at a negotiation and use it as an opportunity to gather intelligence, we won't make it out of the room – or if we do, we certainly won't get back in again.

SASHA: Is that what happened with Bremer and al-Sadr?

CLERIC: Ha! It was like an Old-Testament prophet talking to a New-Testament prophet. Not the way round you'd suppose.

SASHA: .....?

CLERIC: The Americans still think they can walk in and be welcomed, be trusted, because they're the chosen people. At the same time, their command aren't talking to each other. They talk to the Iraqis more than to each other, but always with a different agenda. It's chaos.

SASHA: And the religious conflict?

CLERIC: Well, in a way there isn't one. It isn't Christian v. Muslim, though the Americans almost make it such by default. Fallujah is Sunni, like the Ba'athists, like Saddam. So they're mistrusted by the Shia and by the Yanks not because they're Muslim but because they're Sunni. The Shias are like Catholics; they have centuries of tradition, a real hierarchy with Ayatollahs and a bureaucracy – mosques with affiliated schools and all that. Sunnis have none of this, they're like Protestants, relying on a purist interpretation of the Qur'an, and without an internal infrastructure. Fallujah's become their centre by default – there's nowhere else, historically. Are you going there?

SASHA: They're not letting journalists in. It's a closed door.

CLERIC: That doesn't usually stop your lot going somewhere.

SASHA: Actually, they needn't bother stopping us. No news agency will insure us or our gear in Fallujah, so my own boss has banned me. Anyway, what should the Americans be doing?

MAJOR: The solution to law and order is simple – we did it in Northern Ireland – joint patrols with the local police. People don't mind the guilty being searched. Unfortunately, we disbanded the Iraqi police a year ago. You have to remember the Pentagon is run by guys who fought in Vietnam. Their instinctive response is still 'take 'em out in an MCO...'.

CLERIC: ...major combat operation...

MAJOR: ...*They* are at war, *we* are fighting a counter-insurgency operation. Plus, of course, there is little or no appetite in the Pentagon or in the White House for substantial change. They go in with immediate victory in mind, not effectual change.

SASHA: And what should they have in mind?

CLERIC: Survival! The Americans aren't just running blindly in; to some extent, the insurgents entice them. Red flags to a lot of bull. There *are* car bombs, there *are* kidnappings, there *are* suicide bombs. I've seen Mujahedin with limbs ready-tourniqueted in case of injury. Some people in Fallujah are dangerous.

MAJOR: You see, a leader is a guardian of an idea. It's a quaint notion, but a true one. Fundamentally, wars are about ideas – even if the idea is merely conquest for its own sake. And in Iraq it's a moot point whether a secular, democratic West-leaning Iraq is the right idea to be fighting for. We don't have a winning idea; democracy here is simply impossible. And this has been denied. It has led to terrible planning, and the fundamental experience of Iraqis is one of humiliation and shame. Consequently, we've managed to unite all the various anti-coalition forces against us. We've given them common cause.

SASHA: You're very candid. Thank you.

MAJOR: Well, ultimately Sasha the British aren't involved in this one. It's an American cock-up. My view is that the Americans' use of violence is not proportionate and is over-responsive to the threat they are facing. They don't see the Iraqi people the way we see them. They view them as *untermenschen*. They are not concerned about the Iraqi loss of life. As far as they are concerned Iraq is bandit country and everybody is out to kill them. It is trite, but American troops do shoot first and ask questions later. For God's sake, most Americans can't tell the difference between Iraq and Iran. Perhaps war is God's way of teaching Americans geography.

CLERIC: You have to look also at how they treat their own. In the British army, roughly 3 per cent of soldiers are leaving this war with significant psychiatric problems. In the American army, the figure is over 30 per cent. They're under-trained, under-supported, and nearly underage – their average age is 18, ours is a decade older.

SASHA: And for what?

CLERIC: Ah, the million-dollar question. I don't know. Maybe it's capitalism confronting religion; free-market democracy versus repression. Maybe it is, as has been thought, a clash of fundamentalisms. Maybe it's old-fashioned imperialism and conquest. But I think: look for the dominant idea. Remember, it's a taught process, not a thought process. Even madmen, who hear voices in the air, are usually distilling their frenzy from some defunct ideology of the past. Sooner or later it is ideas, not the vested interests that are their progeny, which are dangerous. Look for the idea.

SASHA: And so? What is happening now?

CLERIC: It's all going to hell in a handcart. Go to Fallujah. You'll see. There's a woman there you should meet, she's been acting as a witness there for months. Jo, her name is.

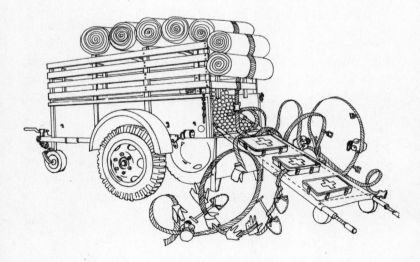

ACT TWO

SCENE 6. Fallujah.

JO walks on, one hand raised, the other holding a loud-hailer. With her is RANA.

RANA: Jo, careful...

JO: Hold your fire! We're here to deliver medical supplies and a new ambulance! I'm English! The vehicle you will see is a new ambulance; it's safe!

(Bullets ricochet around them; they dart back to the wall and wait. The shooting stops.)

JO: Stop shooting! I know you can hear me! We're meant to be on the same side for Christ's sake! These supplies need to get through – people are dying!

(They edge out again. So far so good. They make it further out into the open before the shooting starts again; heavier fire than before. Again they dart back.)

JO (*furious*): You fuckers! If it was your sister in there would you still shoot at us? If it was your apple-pie Mom would you stop us delivering medicine?

(Her companion suddenly crumples.)

JO: Oh, shit (*runs over and cradles her in her lap*). Where? Where've they got you? Tell me where?

RANA: It's OK, they missed me. Jo, we must go.

JO: OK. (*To soldiers*) You bastards! What the fuck was the point of that? Feel better, do you?

RANA: Come on, Jo. Don't antagonize them. We'll find the commander and sort this out. Come. (*They leave.*)

SCENE 7: ONSCREEN ONLY.

SASHA enters and once again watches the footage.

RANA (ONSCREEN): The evidence I've seen about that; I mean I've seen it, not even someone told me about it. When I went looking for a woman, left with a blind old man in the house, we enter into the house, start calling her – no reply. We went out and I said let's look in other houses, but I just noticed something in the garden and it was a body but I couldn't really recognize it, and it looked really bad – it was a body with the colour green, and I have never seen this in all my life, and my work is dealing with dead bodies and all this stuff, but I never seen a body with a green colour.

CUT TO:

PENTAGON SPOKESMAN (ONSCREEN): Napalm has not been used in Iraq. We use Mark 77 incendiary. The US took napalm out of service in the 1970s. We completed the destruction of our last batch of napalm on 4 April 2001, and no longer maintain any stocks of napalm.

SCENE 8: SASHA. Baghdad. 5 April 2004.

SASHA switches off the report and the lighting changes; she turns into this new scene. The scene begins as an apparent soliloquy; we realize only towards the end that she is filing a report.

SASHA: The first news released on the attack referred to the men killed as 'contractors', and even showed an Iraqi man handling the dog tags of one of them; another man was holding a Department of Defense badge from another of the US fighters the Iraqis had killed. The same report mentioned that a collection of weapons was in one of the vehicles as well.

That was the last of that footage I saw. From then on, it was 'Americans killed by Iraqis!' or 'Contractors Killed', over and over *ad nauseum*.

It transpires that these 'Americans killed by Iraqis' happened to be four mercenaries working for a N.C. Security Firm called Blackwater Security Consulting. This subcontractor, along with countless others, is working to provide 'security' in Iraq. They even provide training for SWAT teams and former special operations personnel.

Blackwater Security Consulting won a $35.7 million contract to train over 10,000 soldiers from several states in the US in the art of 'force protection'. They also hire mercenaries from South Africa and other countries as well, and the pay in Iraq is $1,000 per day. US soldiers earn a little over that each month. There are over 20,000 mercenaries in Iraq today – the largest single force in the conflict after the US military, and the largest private army in history. They are accountable to no government and no ideology. They kill for the highest bidder.

So the residents of Fallujah are about to be 'pacified' because some of the resistance fighters there killed what were most likely mercenaries who regularly attack and detain residents of Fallujah. The fog of war grows thicker in Iraq, as the privatization contracts continue to be signed.

CAMERAMAN: Great, Sasha. Obviously we can't use it, but great. (*Exits.*)

CLERIC (*who has been loitering throughout*): Good speech. Will it get used?

SASHA: No. They won't air it; too, er, passionate. Or something more important will displace it – my last report was sidelined in favour of Rebecca Loos wanking a pig. Oh, shit – sorry... Where did you spring from anyway?

CLERIC: Oh, you know, the shadows... How're you doing?

SASHA: Honestly? Not brilliantly. Exhausted, actually. I've been embedded outside Baghdad for a month. Most of the time, I'm crammed in the back of the same Humvee – more bullet holes in it daily. I peer out in time to see pick-ups piled with dead people everywhere I go.

CLERIC: They want you dead. The locals – some of them, at any rate. You know that? It's OK being sympathetic – they're in a mess, no doubt – but they want you to stop breathing. Preferably sooner rather than later.

SASHA: I've developed a strange relationship with the sight of dead Iraqis. I feel safer when I see them. That's shitty, right? I feel especially comforted when I see dead men lying by the side of the road still clutching weapons. Even dead women, now, are a numb relief. They won't be trying to kill me today.

CAMERAMAN (*re-entering*): Sasha, we go now.

SASHA: Yes. We go now.

CLERIC: Look after yourself.

SCENE 9: AUDIO ONLY: An interview with a recently released French journalist.

For the moment, we are unclear to the source of this, it hovers 'above' the action as it were. Scene 10 happens simultaneously.

INTERVIEWER: Maybe I can start by asking you, what were you doing in Iraq, what was your job?

LUCE: At that time we have already made a book...written a book about Saddam, the regime of Saddam, and I was based in Amman as a freelance correspondent for the French Radio, and when the war start I went covering the event. So I was making, you know, a trip...small trip from Amman to Baghdad every month.

INTERVIEWER: Now what happened?

LUCE: Thanks to God at the moment of the hijacking there was no violence. Immediately I said we are French journalists.

I show my press card, it was in Arabic. So they can see immediately we are journalists because the most important thing, when you are held hostage is the first hour. You don't know if they are thief, if they are terrorist, if they are...you don't know, and you could be killed immediately.

So with the press card in Arabic, you know... the tensions go down a little. So, at this time you save your life for a moment, after you don't know, but at this time you feel – phew. OK, I'm not dead yet.

SCENE 10: AT THE SAME TIME AS SCENE 9:
Double-tapping. Fallujah. 2004.

It is important that this is precisely matched to the audio scene above.

An Iraqi man crawls across the floor. He is badly wounded. Exhausted, he slumps to the floor. An American soldier walks on and sees him. After a moment the soldier walks over and looks down at him. Efficiently, he pulls out a pistol and shoots him twice in the head. On his way out he sees a body, obviously dead. Again, he shoots it twice in the head.

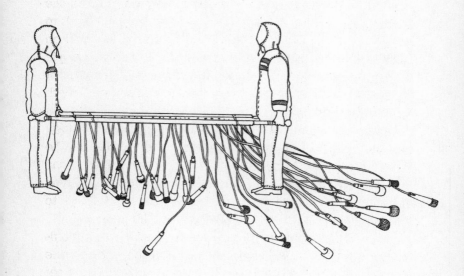

SCENE 11: The assault. Fallujah.

The stage goes black, and heavy metal music is played very, very loudly. There is also the sound of artillery and small arms fire. This should last only for a minute or two.

SCENE 12: THE SNIPER.

He should materialize as close as possible from the audience and, like RANA earlier, address them directly.

SNIPER: Fallujah is a sniper's dream. You can go anywhere and there are so many ways to fire at the enemy without him knowing where you are. It's heaven.

As a sniper your goal is to completely demoralize the enemy. Sometimes a guy will go down, and I'll let him scream a bit to destroy the morale of his buddies. Then I'll use a second shot. I don't really think of these people as people, and I don't know if they're all Fallujans or foreigners. It's hard to tell the nationality of someone with a towel on their face.

I couldn't have asked to be in a better place. I just got lucky: to be here at the right time and with the right training. The first time you get the adrenalin rush afterward. During the shooting, you have to take care of your breathing. It felt good to do my job, good to take a bad guy out. Every time I get to kill someone, he's no longer shooting at the Marines.

I hope we'll be home by Fall, though. I wanna see my girl-friend. After all of this, I wanna coach high school. Continue to give something back. Get married, coach, go deer hunting with my father. When I go hunting for whitetail back home, it's for food and sport. Here, when I go hunting, it's personal. Very personal.

SCENE 13: The Moldovans. 6 April 2004. Baghdad. Another press briefing.

At this point things should begin to appear subtly height-ened, perhaps via the soundscape and the lighting.

SASHA: General, in view of the bombings in Madrid last month, and the decision of the Spanish and other govern-ments to remove troops from Iraq, just how genuinely multi-national is the coalition force at present?

GENERAL: We stand shoulder to shoulder with many allies; there are troops of all nationalities here with us.

SASHA: Yes, but excluding the private contractors – how many sovereign forces are currently in the country? I saw you in discussion with an Eastern European commander earlier today for example, but I couldn't pick out his nationality –

GENERAL: That was our ally the Moldovan General.

SASHA: How exotic. And just how many Moldovan troops are in this theatre at the current time?

GENERAL: I couldn't say for sure, you'd have to ask the General. I know they've had some adjustments to their deployment –

SASHA: They've gone home?

GENERAL: No, there is a reduced force currently –

SASHA: How many troops?

GENERAL: As I say –

SASHA: General, how many?

GENERAL: Well, I believe, er, twelve. Look, goddammit, two years from now, only the Brits may be with us. At some point, we may be the only ones left. That's OK with me. We are America.

SASHA: Twelve.

SECOND JOURNALIST: General, we have heard reports that members of the press have been prevented from reporting and that news channels have been shut down. Could you comment?

GENERAL: Al-Jazeera was responsible for vicious and inaccurate reporting. The channel was inciting hatred, and had to be closed down.

SECOND JOURNALIST: And the others?

GENERAL: Look, the stations that are showing Americans killing women and children are not legitimate news sources.

SECOND JOURNALIST: And if people come across such footage, if it gets reported, if they see what's happening here; what should we tell them then?

GENERAL: Tell them to change the channel.

SECOND JOURNALIST: General, could you comment on the detainment of the French journalists by US troops last week, in which they were bound and blindfolded and treated like POWs?

GENERAL: I would dispute the allegations most seriously.

SECOND JOURNALIST: The troops filmed their humiliation with the reporters' own cameras. The footage has been screened on French television.

GENERAL: No comment.

SECOND JOURNALIST: How far would you consider taking the gagging of news agencies? Would you bomb a station like Al-Jazeera?

GENERAL: No more questions.

SCENE 14: Kidnapping. Fallujah.

JO is sitting on a wooden bench. Next to her is AHRAR. Both are captives. By their side is an Iraqi man with a Kalashnikov.

MAN: Do not worry. We will not hurt you. You are safe. (*Beat.*) What is your name?

AHRAR: Ahrar.

MAN: And you?

JO: Jo.

MAN: And what do you do in Iraq, Jo?

JO: I help to get medical supplies to hospitals. The Americans usually don't shoot if they see a white face.

MAN: And what do you do when not in Iraq?

JO: I'm an entertainer. I entertain children. I suppose I'm a clown.

MAN (*beat*): You are in the wrong city.

JO: Yes. Please, let us go?

MAN: No. It is not safe. If we release you, others will take you. Others not so good.

JO: Why us? Why take us?

MAN: My brother was killed and my brother's son and my sister's son. My other brother is in the prison at Abu Ghraib. I am the last one left. Can you imagine? And this morning my best friend was killed. He was wounded in the leg and lying in the street and the Americans came and cut his throat. Now, tell me, why us? Is it another crusade? First, they wanted Saddam. Was my brother Saddam? Now they say they search for Zarqawi. Are the children they shoot Zarqawi? Are the people they napalm Zarqawi? This is our Hiroshima.

JO: I'm sorry. We are trying to help.

MAN: I know that. That is why we will let you go. But not now. In the morning, when it is light. (*He is about to leave, and stops.*) You know, Fallujah people like peace but after we were attacked the US lost all their friends here. We had a few trained officers and soldiers from the old army, but now everyone has joined the effort. We are willing to fight until the last minute, even if it takes a hundred years. Why did you not talk to us? You see, even here, I am talking to you. (*He leaves.*)

AHRAR: Oh God, Oh God.

JO: It's OK, try to stay calm.

AHRAR: Oh, God, Oh God.

JO: They say they won't hurt us.

AHRAR: It's not them – it's Mama. What will she say when I won't come home tonight? And I'm with English people! Oh God! She'll kill me!

JO: Oh. Yes I see. I'm so sorry for getting you into this. (*Pause.*) We'll be OK, I promise.

AHRAR: You don't know Mama! (*Pause*) I told you they were Muja.

JO: I know, but Marines were in the same location yesterday, so the choice was either not to wave and be shot, if they were Marines, or wave and get captured, if they were Muja.

AHRAR: I know. You were right. Where is your passport?

JO: In my bra. I think it's safe there.

MAN (*re-entering*): Come now. We will take you. It is time.

JO (*trying to be courageous*): It will not help you if you kill us. You know that. (*Man moves towards her.*) A minute; do you have children? (*Man hesitates. Slowly JO pulls from her pocket a balloon. Expertly she blows it up and twists it into a balloon animal, before offering it to the man. They both stare at it for a moment.*)

JO: No. Perhaps not.

Fade to black.

JO (*voiceover*): What do you do when you're kidnapped in Iraq? What do you do? You look for ways out. You wonder whether they're going to kill you, make demands for your release, if they'll hurt you. You wait for the knives and the guns and the video camera. You tell yourself you're going to be OK. You think about your family, your mum finding out you're kidnapped. You decide you're going to be strong, because there's nothing else you can do. You fight the understanding that your life isn't fully in your hands any more, that you can't control what's happening. You decide you won't cry, that you'll look directly at the guy in charge if the time comes. You turn to your best friend next to you and you tell her you love her, you love her, with all your heart and more.

(*As the voiceover ends the women start singing – this time something RANA can join in with. After a time the singing stops and the sound of morning prayers fades in. For a while this is all that can be heard.*)

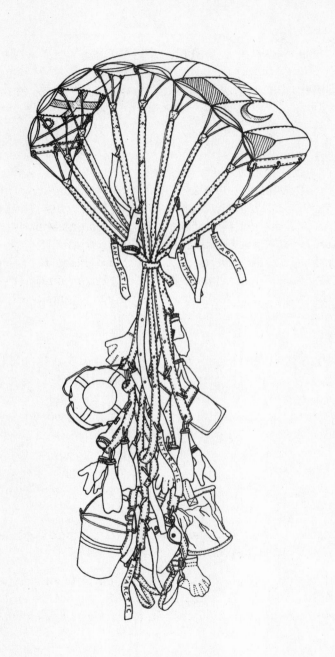

ACT THREE

SCENE 15: In the USA. A speech in Stanford.

As with Scene 1, this should begin as if the audience are actually entering to hear a speech. Possibly RICE is introduced by one of the other actors. All the screens show her speech as she talks, and groups of the cast watch it on small televisions. To emphasize this, the first paragraph is spoken both live and pre-recorded. The lights then dim on RICE – but with no effect on her screen persona – and we watch the other characters watching their TVs (one group perhaps listens on the radio); first one group, then another. The lights come back up on RICE for her final paragraph. Clearly what is happening technically is that the first and final paragraphs are projected live, and the middle section of the speech is pre-recorded.

RICE: If the collapse of the Soviet Union and 9/11 bookend a major shift in international politics, then this is a period not just of grave danger, but of enormous opportunity. Before the clay is dry again, America and our friends and our allies must move decisively to take advantage of these new opportunities. This is, then, a period akin to 1945 to 1947, when American leadership expanded the number of free and democratic states to create a new balance of power that favoured freedom.

Lights dim on RICE, and up on one group to stage left (or right), digesting the speech on TV.

It is, indeed, possible to see age-old problems in a new light. And, as an academic, may I suggest, to put aside age-old distinctions between realism and neoliberalism in thinking about the task ahead. Put more simply than any of its proponents would find acceptable, realists downplay the importance of values and the internal structures of states, emphasizing instead the balance of power as the key to stability and peace. Neoliberals emphasize the primacy of values, such as freedom and democracy and human rights and institutions, in ensuring that a just political order is obtained.

Lights dim on first group, and up on another group to stage right (or left), digesting the speech on radio.

As a professor, I recognize that these debates enliven our conferences and our classrooms. (*Laughter.*) I have participated in them, myself. In fact, most of us got tenure because we participated in them. (*Laughter.*) But as a policymaker, I can tell you that they obscure reality. Power matters. Great powers matter. Great powers never have, and never will just mind their own business within their borders.

Lights up again on RICE.

Europe and the United States see that our common and fundamental interests and values far outweigh our differences. When people are trying to kill you, and when they attack because they hate freedom, other disputes – from Franken-food to bananas to even important issues like the environment – suddenly look a bit different. They look like policy differences, not fundamental clashes of values. A balance of power that favours freedom is, at its core, a balance of power based on the ascendancy of shared values on every continent.

Lights down on listening groups.

America cannot impose its vision on the world – yet, we will use our influence to favour freedom. There are right and wrong choices and right and wrong acts. And governments are making them every day for their own people and for the people of the world. We can never let the intricacies of cloistered debate – with its many hues of grey and nuance – obscure the need to speak and act with moral clarity. We must recognize that some states or leaders will choose wrongly. We must recognize that truly evil regimes will never be reformed. And we must recognize that such regimes must be confronted, not coddled. It is not the people we fight, it is the regime.

SCENE 16: The Trade Fair. Baghdad.

The cast, already in the space, leap to life and mingle with the audience. The following is fast and furious, with each cast member contributing a line. The screen follows the dialogue with a stream of logos etc.

- It'll be only a matter of months until Starbucks and McDonald's open branches in Baghdad.
- HSBC will have cash machines all over the country.
- Getting the rights to distribute Procter & Gamble can be a goldmine.
- One well-stocked 7-Eleven could knock out thirty Iraqi stores.
- A Wal-Mart could take over the country.
- Relax and celebrate victory.
- It's kind of bad we destroyed everything, but at least we gave them a chance for a new start.
- The predictions of those who opposed this war can be discarded like spent cartridges.

- We ought to look in a mirror and get proud and stick out our chests and suck in our bellies and say: 'Damn, we're Americans'.

- Iraq would be fine if the Iraqis just washed their hands and cleaned the crap off the walls.

- With a heavy dose of fear and violence, and a lot of money for projects, I think we can convince these people that we are here to help them.

- Next year at about this time, I expect there will be a really thriving trade in the region, and we will see rapid economic development.

- And a year from now, I'll be very surprised if there is not some grand square in Baghdad named after President Bush.

- I don't think Iraq will have perfect elections. But, if I recall, looking back at our own election four years ago, it wasn't perfect either.

- Death has a tendency to encourage a depressing view of war.

- An Iraqi said to me yesterday, 'Why us?' He had no understanding that we are here to protect his country. All he needs to do is understand that we know best, and he'll be safe.

ANNOUNCER: Gentleman, the New Bridges Strategies trade fair, for the first time taking place in Baghdad, is about to begin. Please welcome our distinguished guest and plenary speaker, a man who exemplifies what it is to be a true American in both business and politics; Gentlemen, I give you – Mr Arnold Schwarzenegger!

SCENE 17: ONSCREEN ONLY.

This should overlap with the previous scene, and act as a bridge into the more straightforwardly staged scene that comes next. Again, SASHA initiates it by switching on the TV.

RANA (ONSCREEN): And later I met a guy with experience in these things and he say this is the chemical weapons that they use. It was a civilian – I can tell the fighter from the dress. This was a civilian, and there was a white flag in the garden. It was a man, early fifties, late forties.

They used these weird bombs that put up smoke like a mushroom cloud. Then small pieces fell from the air with long tails of smoke behind them. Pieces of these bombs exploded into large fires that burnt peoples' skin even when water was dumped on their bodies. People suffered so much from these, both civilians and fighters alike. There is a terrible crime going in Fallujah and they do not want anybody to know.

CUT TO:

CORPORATE SPOKESWOMAN (ONSCREEN): The difference? Napalm-B is Mark 47, now we use Mark 77. The inflammable fuel in Mark 77 firebombs is thickened with slightly different chemicals, and contains oxidizers, which make it harder to extinguish than Napalm-B. In short, Mark 77 does the job better. Here at Rock Island Arsenal, in Illinois, our facility is currently producing a further 500 Mark 77s for the US Marine Corps.

SCENE 18: The Checkpoint. The road to Fallujah.

SASHA: You won't let us through?

SOLDIER: Can't. Orders. No press. Get back or you'll get killed

SASHA: Look, I'm not here as press. I'm an academic. I'm here to find another, fellow academic – an Englishwoman, Jo... – who is trapped in Fallujah. I've checked with General Mendez, we can go through. Please, call him yourself.

SOLDIER: You know I can't just call up a General. (*Pause. Gives up.*) Oh, OK – you can go. But I have your ID and I will be checking.

SASHA: Thank you. Thanks so much.

SOLDIER: By the way, you don't have to wear those things anymore (*hijabs*); you're liberated now!

SASHA: We wouldn't have had to wear them before. Now we do.

SOLDIER: Well, you guys be careful in Fallujah, you hear? We're killing loads of those folks. (*Pause.*) Well, they're killing us too. I like Fallujah. I killed a bunch of those motherfuckers myself.

SASHA: The General announced that anyone leaving the city would be considered non-dangerous. Are you letting anyone out?

SOLDIER: Oh, we want to keep them in there. There's fighters coming from all over Iraq to here and we want to keep them all in there so we can kill them all more easily.

(A mortar is heard close by. SASHA jumps.)

SOLDIER: Don't worry. It's outgoing.

SASHA: That's comforting. Though I can't help but think it has RSVP written all over it. Thanks again.

SOLDIER: Pleasure. Jeez it's good to meet someone that speaks English instead of speaking in tongues. Well, apart from 'Mister' and 'please' and 'why'.

SASHA: Don't you have translators?

SOLDIER *(lifts his rifle)*: I got the best translator in the world. You have a nice day, now, you hear?

SCENE 19: Fallujah. 7 April.

The next four scenes should run speedily and energetically, as a unit in themselves. The effect should be quite disorienting.

LIEUTENANT *(to his men)*: Collective punishment is imposed on the people of Fallujah by those terrorists and cowards that hunker down inside mosques, hospitals and schools and use women and children as shields to hide. Expect snipers on all minarets, all towers. They will do it to draw fire and cause collateral damage in the hour of prayer. They want the streets to run with our blood.

Now, if we can find a peaceful way out of this, then great – someone just tell me what it is. But at this point there seem to be few options other than to level this town, wipe it clear off the map.

We are confronting the evildoers who have a grasp on this country. The 60,000 people who have left Fallujah have by doing so agreed that the terrorists and criminals in their city have to be eliminated. The intention is not to take the town of Fallujah; our intent is to give the town of Fallujah back to the Fallujan people. The only way to do this is to go in with heavy armour, and to kill people.

To be clear: you will be held accountable for the facts not as they are in hindsight but as they appeared to you at the time. If, in your mind, you fire to protect yourself or your men, you are doing the right thing. It doesn't matter if later on we find out you wiped out a family of unarmed civilians.

There's a picture of the Twin Towers hanging up by my bed and I keep one in my Kevlar. Every time I feel sorry for these people I look at that. I think, 'They hit us at home and now it's our turn'. We're going out where the bad guys live, and we're going to slay them in their ZIP code. It's payback time. People have said we confront a faceless enemy. But I say the enemy has got a face, the enemy has a name. He's called Satan. He's in Fallujah and we are going to destroy him.

SCENE 20: Checkpoint, dusk.

RANA is attempting to leave Fallujah before it all kicks off. The Iraqi National Guard (ING) won't allow it.

(In Arabic.)

RANA: You have to let me out. It's dangerous in here after dark. You know this.

ING: Then you know you should have left before now.

RANA: What's your problem? You want me to get killed? Why are you doing this?

ING: You stay where you are, bitch.

(*A US soldier appears.*)

SOLDIER: What's going on here? Rana, is that you? What are you doing here so late. You wanna get shot?

RANA: This fucking Iraqi National Guard, he won't let me through, I'm trapped for the night.

SOLDIER: Hey, man, why're you not letting her through?

ING: We are in charge here. She cannot leave.

RANA: My daily suffering is these checkpoints with the Iraqi National Guard. They give me such shit, accuse me of helping terrorists, they don't want anyone to help the Fallujans.

SOLDIER: I saw other guys leave just before here. Why the exception for her? You only letting men out tonight?

ING: Look, is my checkpoint, she stays.

SOLDIER: And this is my authority (*points to the gun*); she leaves, and you shut the fuck up. (*To RANA*) Watch your ass, I'll escort you back to the clinic in the morning.

SCENE 21: ATTACK. Fallujah.

Excruciating noise. The soldiers leave, and SASHA and a few civilians cower in terror. Explosions repeat and are punctuated with white noise – so-called 'noise bombs' –

which is unbearable. Gunshots, mortars and machine gun fire are heard and clearly unarmed civilians collapse. We run the aural gamut of a bombardment, though we see very little. This goes on for several minutes before subsiding.

SCENE 22: AFTERMATH. Fallujah.

SASHA is clearly very shaken. Much of what she describes can be heard taking place throughout the speech.

SASHA: This is what I found in Fallujah. The Iraqi National Guard used loudspeakers to call on people to get out of the houses carrying white flags, bringing all their belongings with them. They were ordered to gather outside near the Jamah al-Furkan mosque in the centre of town. Eight members of Eyad Naji Latif's family – one of them a six-month-old child – gathered their belongings and walked in single file, as instructed, to the mosque. (*We hear this taking place, but the stage remains bare.*)

When they reached the main road outside the mosque they heard a shout, but they could not understand what was being shouted. A Red Crescent doctor told me it could have been 'now' in English.

DOCTOR (*interviewed by SASHA*): Then the firing began. US soldiers appeared on the roofs of surrounding houses and opened fire. Eyad's father was shot in the heart and his mother in the chest. They died instantly. Two of Eyad's brothers were also hit, one in the chest and one in the neck. Two of the women were hit, one in the hand and one in the leg. Then the snipers killed the wife of one of Eyad's brothers. When she fell her five-year-old son ran to her and stood over her body. They shot him dead too.

Survivors made desperate appeals to the troops to stop firing. But whenever one of them tried to raise a white flag they were shot. After several hours Eyad tried to raise his arm with the flag. But they shot him in the arm. Finally he tried to raise his hand. So they shot him in the hand.

The five survivors, including the six-month-old child, lay in the street, surrounded by the blood of their families, for seven hours. Then four of them crawled to the nearest home to find shelter. The next morning the brother who was shot in the neck also managed to crawl to safety. They all stayed in the house for eight days, surviving on roots and one cup of water, which they saved for the baby. On the eighth day they were discovered by some members of the Iraqi National Guard and taken to hospital in Fallujah.

SASHA: The US military at first refused to hand over bodies of fighters to be buried, and when they did, many were half-eaten by dogs.

(*An American officer passes across the stage and pauses.*)

LIEUTENANT: When we hit the mosque I thought we had killed all the bad guys, but when we went in they didn't find any bad guys in the building.

SCENE 23: The Grunts.

SOLDIERS enter, retreating from a bombardment.

SOLDIER 1: What's our situation, Sir?

LIEUTENANT: Our situation is good. The enemy is coming to us. And we're killing him. (*Exits.*)

The conversation is half between themselves and half with the audience: they mingle with the audience as they talk. The first part of the scene should be fast and furious, with dialogue overlapping and speakers interjecting.

SOLDIER 2: The fight lasted for about eight hours and they just kept on coming all day from everywhere, from all sides. All in plain clothes.

SOLDIER 3: We had dropped fliers a couple of days prior saying to people to get out of the area if they didn't want to fight, so basically anyone who was there was a combatant. If they were dumb enough to stand in front of tanks or drive a car towards a tank, then they were there to fight. On that day it took away the dilemma of who to fire at, anyone who was there was a combatant.

SOLDIER 2: That day nothing went with the training. There were females fighting; there were some that, when they saw you fucking coming, they'd just drop their shit and try to give up; and some guys were shot and they'd fucking play dead, and when you'd go by they'd reach for their weapons.

SOLDIER 1: That day it was just fucking everything. When we face women or injured that try to grab their weapons, we just finish them off. You've gotta, no choice.

SOLDIER 2: The worst thing is to shoot one of them, then go help him. In that situation you're angry, you're raging. They'd just been hiding in shops and up towers, shooting at my men – they were putting my guys in a casket and eight feet under, that's what they were trying to do. And now, they're laying there and I have to help them, I have a responsibility to ensure my men help them?

SOLDIER 1: Shit, I didn't help any of them. I wouldn't help the fuckers. There were some you let die. And there were some you double-tapped. (*Makes a double-shooting noise while pointing his hand at the floor.*)

SOLDIER 3: I mean, what do people think happens when they tell us to assault a city? Marines don't shoot rainbows out of our asses. We fucking kill people. I mean, people want their steak but they don't wanna hear how the cow gets slaughtered, you know, see the blood?

SOLDIER 2: Once you'd reached the objective, and once you'd shot them and you're moving through, anything there, you shoot again. You didn't want any prisoners of war. You hate them so bad while you're fighting, and you're so terrified, you can't really convey the feeling, but you don't want them to live.

SOLDIER 3: At night you think about all the people you killed. It just never gets off your head, none of this stuff does. There's no chance to forget it, we're still here, we've been here so long. Most people leave after combat but we haven't. I mean, why the fuck us?

SOLDIER 1: Some soldiers don't even fucking sleep at night. They sit up all fucking night long doing shit to keep themselves busy – to keep their minds off this fucking stuff. It's the only way they can handle it. It's not so far from being crazy but it's their way of coping. There's one guy trying to build a little pool out the back, pointless stuff but it keeps him busy.

SOLDIER 3: For me, it's like snap-shot photos. Like pictures of maggots on tongues, babies with their heads on the ground, men with their heads halfway off and their eyes wide open and mouths wide open. Blood all over. Do you know how much a body bleeds? The whole country flooded with blood. Not even the fucking gulf could wash it off. I see it every day, every single day. The smells and the torsos burning. Nothing but burned bodies.

SOLDIER 2: There are bodies that we saw when we went back to secure a place we'd taken. The bodies were still there and they'd been baking in the sun. Their bodies were bloated three times the size.

SOLDIER 1: Now we're in this peacekeeping, we're always firing off a warning shot at people that don't wanna listen to you. They don't wanna speak your language, just babble at you. You make up the rules as you go along.

SOLDIER 3: Like, in Fallujah we get rocks thrown at us by kids. You wanna turn round and shoot one of the little fuckers. But you know you can't do that. Their parents know if they came out and threw rocks we'd shoot them. So that's why they send the kids out.

SOLDIER 2: You go and fight that war, and you win decisively, but now you have to stay and stabilize the situation. We are having to go from a full war-fighting mindset to a peacekeeping mindset overnight.

SOLDIER 1: Right after shooting at people who were trying to kill you, you now have to help them.

SOLDIER 2: We weren't trained for this stuff now. It makes you resentful they're holding us on here. It pisses everyone

off, we were told once the war was over we'd leave when
our replacements get here. Well, our replacements got here
and we're still here.

SOLDIER 3: We're more angry at the generals who are
making these decisions and who never hit the ground,
and who don't get shot at or have to look at the bloody
bodies and the burnt-out bodies, and the dead babies
and all that kinda stuff. They say 'God bless us'. Where
the fuck did Jesus say it's OK to kill people for your
government?

SOLDIER 2: Americans celebrate war in their movies.
We like to see visions of evil being defeated by good.
When the people at home glimpse the reality of war, that
it's a bloodbath, they freak out. We are a subculture they
created and programmed to fight their wars. You have
to become a psycho to kill like we do. To most Marines
a wounded guy is just someone who didn't get hit in the
right place the first time we shot him. If the American
public doesn't like the violence of war, they shouldn't be
in such a rush to endorse the next one.

SOLDIER 1: I don't care about Iraq one way or the other.
I couldn't care less. Saddam could still be in power and, to
me, it wasn't worth leaving my family for; for getting shot
at and almost dying two or three times, there's nothing
worth that to me. Fucking hell, it's not about nations or
regimes; it's about people.

SCENE 24: AUDIO ONLY. French interview.

During this scene the hospital for the next one comes into being.

INTERVIEWER: And then what happened, they sent somebody senior to you and what did he tell you?

LUCE: He explained that we were... it was two days after the hijack... the Chief of the Intelligence of the Islamic Army in Iraq came to us, he was a fat man, maybe he was working with Saddam at the same place, and he explained us: 'We are between 15 and 17,000 soldier and we are fighting four fronts, America and British troops occupation. We are against the spy and also the Iraqi police' and he said to us: 'We have infiltrated also the police, so we are Sunni' and it was a kind of presentation.

So for us it was important because they have a political agenda, so they are not crazy you know. So they have the logic, even if it's cruel and awful, but they have a sense of either you are with them or against them, like Bush – with him or against him, it's the same.

Ten days after the same guy, the fat guy: 'Your case is frozen because we have problems in Fallujah, Americans are preparing a big offensive, a big attack on Fallujah, so all our troops are going there so your case is frozen, but by the way, what do you think about the Islamic veil in France?'

INTERVIEWER: So that's the message you put on the video.

LUCE: Exactly.

ACT FOUR

SCENE 25: The clinic. Fallujah.

There are people, tired and harassed, trying to care for people on stretchers, with rudimentary tourniquets and no real equipment. The DOCTOR brings in SASHA.

DOCTOR: They entered the theatre room when we were working on a patient. They entered with their boots on, beat the doctors and took them out, leaving the patient on the table to die.

In the first week of the siege, they bombed the Hay Nazal clinic. This contained all the foreign aid and medical instruments we had. All the US military commanders knew this, because we told them about it so they wouldn't bomb it. But this was one of the clinics bombed, and in the first week of the siege they bombed it two times. Of course they targeted all our ambulances and doctors. Everyone knows this. Now, there are no surgeons in Fallujah, and only a handful of general practitioners and nurses.

This is Jo. Jo is from Bristol. She's been here and in Baghdad. She helps us. She'll show you around.

JO: Hello.

SASHA: Hi.

RANA: Hi.

JO (*showing SASHA around*): It's not a hospital at all but a clinic, a private doctor's surgery treating people for free since air strikes destroyed the town's main hospital. Another has been improvised in a car garage. There's no anaesthetic. The blood bags are in a drinks fridge and the doctors warm them up under the hot tap in the toilet.

SASHA: Why? I mean, why these people?

RANA: It's the corporations; it's not the Americans. We are in this together, against the corporations. They are working together – they want no educated people in the world, they want KFC burgers, lying watching TV. Remember, Iraq was one of the best-educated countries in the world, not just in the Middle East. We used to have free education up to university graduation; free health care. Now they find division where there isn't any. The Americans bring Shia police to Fallujah, which is another way to create a civil war. And that's it. They did it for a purpose, to bring Shia militia to Fallujah, which is typically Sunni. Why? You tell me.

(They busy themselves around the 'ward' during the following.)

SCENE 26: AUDIO ONLY, French interview.

INTERVIEWER: Now, in late September you were transferred again into another cell.

LUCE: It was completely different. In this house we are living with five Mujahedin, making operation against the American. So we have lots of discussion with them and especially one, we call him the Jihadist, you know, he was very close to Bin Laden, he was trained in Afghanistan with Bin Laden. He didn't say Bin Laden, he said: 'Sheikh Osama', it was a respectful word. He said: 'I have been fighting in Bosnia' and we saw he has a kind of charisma comparing to the other.

And it's not theatre, it's life, it's death or life, so you don't cheat, so you are... So it was up and down, and so you have to be strong, you try to cope. It's not normal to be on stage you know, and if someone has stumbled before you on your stage I say how can I survive, you know, and finally you survive. Because it's the instinct of life. It's a kind of...you know...a physical principle you know.

SCENE 27. JO and RANA. Interviewed by SASHA.

Throughout this the soundscape presents some of what she talks of – the bullets, the car being hit. One of the other female actors begins to sing towards the end.

SASHA (*to camera, a report*): Jo had been helping where she could, acting as a human passport, witnessing.

The clinic is madness. Screaming women come in, praying, slapping their chests and faces. 'Ummi' – my mother – one cries. I hold her until Maki, the acting direc-tor of the clinic, brings me to the bed where a child of about ten is lying with a bullet wound to the head. A smaller child is being treated for a similar injury in the next bed. A US sniper hit them and their grandmother as they left their home to flee Fallujah.

A body arrives at the hospital; a wound to the man's leg and his throat is sliced open. The men say he was lying injured in the street and the Marines came out and slit his throat. A pick-up races up and a man is pulled out with most of his arm missing, a stump with bits sticking out, pouring blood. He bleeds to death.

The lights go out, the fan stops and in the sudden quiet someone holds up the flame of a cigarette lighter for the doctor to carry on operating by. The electricity to the town has been cut off for days and when the generator runs out of petrol they just have to manage till it comes back on. Rana quickly donates her torch. The children are not going to live.

'Come,' says Maki and ushers me alone into a room where an old woman has just had an abdominal bullet wound stitched up. Another wound in her leg is being dressed, the bed under her foot soaked with blood, a white flag still clutched in her hand and the same story: I was leaving my home to go to Baghdad when I was hit by a US sniper. Some of the town is held by US Marines, other parts by the local fighters. Their homes are in the US-controlled area and they are adamant that the snipers were US Marines.

Snipers are causing not just carnage but also the paralysis of the ambulance and evacuation services. The biggest hospital after the main one was bombed is in US territory and cut off from the clinic by snipers. The ambulance has been repaired four times after bullet damage. Bodies are lying in the streets because no one can go to collect them without being shot. The dew falls red with blood...

(*A swift 'cut' to the three women talking; RANA and JO are being informally interviewed by SASHA.*)

JO: The doctor rushes out to meet me: 'Can you go to fetch a lady, she is pregnant and she is delivering the baby too soon?'

RANA: And the people from the clinic, they tell us: 'If you can't do it, you can't do it'. It's like a suicide mission, crazy.

JO: Azzam is driving, Rana in the middle directing him and me by the window, the visible foreigner, the passport.

Something scatters across my hand, simultaneous with the crashing of a bullet through the ambulance, some plastic part dislodged, flying through the window.

We stop, turn off the siren, keep the blue light flashing, wait, eyes on the silhouettes of men in US marine uniforms on the corners of the buildings. Several shots come. We duck, get as low as possible and I can see tiny red lights whipping past the window, past my head. Some are hitting the ambulance. I start singing. What else do you do when someone's shooting at you? A tyre bursts with an enormous noise and a jerk of the vehicle.

I'm outraged. We're trying to get to a woman who's giving birth without any medical attention, without electricity, in a city under siege, in a clearly marked ambulance, and you're shooting at us. Who is in charge? How can you? Why us? How dare you?

Azzam grabs the gear stick and gets the ambulance into reverse, another tyre bursting as we go over the ridge in the centre of the road, the shots still coming as we flee around the corner. I carry on singing. The wheels are scraping, burst rubber burning on the road.

The men run for a stretcher as we arrive and I shake my head. They spot the new bullet holes and run to see if we're OK. Is there any other way to get to her, I want to know. *La, maaku tarieq.* There is no other way. They say we did the right thing. They say they've fixed the ambulance four times already and they'll fix it again but the radiator's gone and the wheels are buckled and she's still at home in the dark giving birth alone.

We take off the blue gowns as the sky starts exploding somewhere beyond the building opposite. Minutes later a car roars up to the clinic. I can hear him screaming before

I can see that there's no skin left on his body. He's burnt from head to foot. For sure there's nothing they can do. He'll die of dehydration within a few days.

We go again, this time in a pick-up. There are some sick people close to the Marines' line who need evacuating. No one dares come out of their house because the Marines are on top of the buildings shooting at anything that moves. Saad fetches us a white flag and tells us not to worry, he's checked and secured the road, no Mujahedin will fire at us, that peace is upon us, this eleven-year-old child, his face covered with a keffiyeh, but for his bright brown eyes, his AK-47 almost as tall as he is.

We shout again to the soldiers, hold up the flag with a red crescent sprayed onto it. Two come down from the build- ing, cover this side and Rana mutters, '*Allahu akbar*. Please nobody take a shot at them.' We jump down and tell them we need to get some sick people from the houses and they want Rana to go and bring out the family from the house whose roof they're on. Thirteen women and children are still inside, in one room, without food and water for the last twenty-four hours.

RANA: The scary silhouettes of helmets are still on the roof. I help children whose father was shot on his doorstep. I see his body – and their friends, and I walk holding their hands, and I say to one child, 'Your father is OK, he will be at the camp, don't worry'. And the other one, the one holding my other hand, say 'Oh, so my parents will be OK too, then?' and I realize his parents were also dead. It was a really bad moment for me.

JO: Rana's with the Marines evacuating the family from the house they're occupying. The pick-up isn't back yet.

The families are hiding behind their walls. We wait, because there's nothing else we can do. We wait in no man's land. The Marines are watching us through binoculars.

RANA: One of the Americans asked me, 'Do you speak Arabic?' and I can't lie so I say yes, and he said 'come with me'. And that was a terrible thing. All the way down the road and I had no idea what he was going to do with me, where we were going. And this captain walked me all the way down, and he said nothing. And then we reached a house full of women with RPGs, mortars outside. We went into the house and I thought 'Oh my god I'm going to be killed'. And then he opened the door and I saw a woman with kids and he asked me to ask her to leave because it was unsafe for them! And that was one American I did respect. But the woman did not believe me because she thought I was just working for the Americans.

JO: I've got a hanky in my pocket so while I'm sitting like a lemon, nowhere to go, gunfire and explosions aplenty all around, I do tricks – I make the hanky disappear, reappear, disappear. It's always best, I think, to seem completely unthreatening and completely unconcerned, so no one worries about you enough to shoot. They won't listen if you call out to them, even though we share the same language.

The pick-up gets back and we shovel as many onto it as we can as an ambulance arrives from somewhere. It follows us down. The soldiers start shouting in English at us for it to stop, pointing guns. It's moving fast. We're all yelling, signalling for it to stop but Rana seems not to hear or understand our words or see us. The soldiers lift their rifles and take aim – at the ambulance and also at us. Why can't Rana hear us and stop? Time slows. They must shoot. And then the ambulance stops. It stops before they open fire.

We haul more people onto the stretchers and run, shove them in the back. Rana squeezes in the front with the wounded man and I crouch in the back beside the bodies. The stench makes me retch. She says she had allergies as a kid and hasn't got much sense of smell. I wish, retrospectively, for childhood allergies, and stick my head out the window.

RANA: So we get the ambulance through the checkpoint and suddenly we are surrounded by Iraqis, guns pointing, ready to shoot, shouting 'You are traitors, you are taking Americans wounded to the hospital'! I mean, in a shot-up van! And the wounded say 'Hey! We are Fallujans. Which Americans are you talking about? The Americans evacuate the wounded by helicopter, not in vans like these! What are you talking about?' So we got through.

JO: I hate that a medic can't travel in the ambulance but I can, just because I look like the sniper's sister or one of his mates. Azzam keeps asking me if things are going to be OK. '*Al-melaach wiyana,*' I tell him. 'The angels are with us.' He laughs.

SCENE 28. AUDIO ONLY: French interview.

Beneath this scene, work continues at the clinic and the screens show documentary footage of the devastation in Fallujah. Both are cleared by the end of the speech.

INTERVIEWER: So at the end how did you know that you were going to be released?

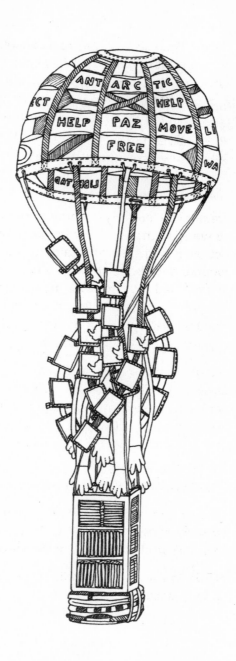

LUCE: It was clear three days before. It was the 18 of December, Saturday, and chief of the intelligence came and said: 'The news are good for you. You are close to your freedom. And he came to make the tape of release. And they give us back the passport and everything, so without any words they didn't go out and they handcuff us, it was not with a rope but with a computer cable, and just before jumping in the car they take out the mask and we were very afraid, say maybe this is the end.

INTERVIEWER: And then?

LUCE: And between fifteen minutes we were very afraid because we were driving on very chaotic road, you know, so maybe we imagined they would kill just then, maybe the negotiations are over and after twenty to twenty-five minutes, the car stopped on a motorway. The door opened and we saw... I saw... I was the first to go out.

I saw the blue sky, I saw the hijackers, the French cars of the Embassy, and the guy it was the chief of the French Intelligence Service. 'Luce, it's over, come here.' I pass and on the way I look, it was like in a film you know, I turned my head and I saw in the eyes my hijacker, he has a keffiyeh and he just... we didn't say anything but it was like in a film, we look at each other and I jump in the car and George was following, and after two minutes we left.

At the end of this scene the voices should fade seamlessly on to track and then on to a tape recorder held by RANA, who switches it off and hands it to SASHA as they move into the next scene. The available interpretation is that all that has gone before has been the result of their reporting, and that we are now in the present.

SCENE 29: The mortuary.

Lights up on AHRAR, SASHA and the DOCTOR. They look around, sombre and shaken, at the bodies on cots.

AHRAR: This is the freedom.

DOCTOR: The morgues in all the hospitals are filling with bodies everyday, most of them shot by soldiers. But also from crime and accidents. So many dead civilians.

SASHA: This is the most horrible thing I've ever seen in my life. I don't know what to do. What do you do?

DOCTOR: I need another heart and eyes to bear it because my own are not enough. Nothing justifies what has been done to this city.

AHRAR: You know it is only going to get worse. Everyday is worse than the last day. Today will be better than tomorrow. Right now is better than the next hour. This is our life here now.

(SASHA turns from a cot, disorientated, and bangs her head. Immediately the doctor holds her head and administers salts.)

SASHA: Thank you.

DOCTOR: My head is spinning also, working here.

SASHA: I want to take a shower.

AHRAR: I wish I could shower from the inside. From the outside it's very easy. But how do we clean from the inside? In Islam, if we touch a dead body, even if we just see one, we should clean.

DOCTOR: Don't think about it. I know it is hard. It is harder on me because I am an Iraqi. My heart is shredding. This is our civilization now.

(SASHA gags.)

SASHA: The smell, oh God. But it's the eyes that get me. And they won't go away. *(Suddenly)* Can I use your phone? It's my birthday.

(AHRAR takes out a phone and fiddles with it.)

AHRAR: They can track the satellite phones even when they're not on, only by removing the SIM card can they not be tracked.

(SASHA takes the phone and begins to text. AHRAR quietly begins to hum 'Happy Birthday'.)

AHRAR: If you don't laugh here, you lose your mind in a hurry.

SASHA *(finishes her message)*: This is the freedom.

(The three women hug.)

AHRAR: Watch your ass and get the hell out of here, habibi.

SCENE 30: A press conference, Baghdad.

SASHA *(reporting to camera)*: As of June 2005 Fallujans say that approximately 100,000 people are still refugees, unable to return to their homes, many of which no longer exist. Most people in the city continue to live in tents, or amid the rubble of their homes. Fallujah has become Iraq, and

Iraq now is Fallujah. Residents were allowed to return to the city after undergoing biometric identification, provided they wear their ID cards all the time.

Almost 36,000 houses have been demolished, 9,000 shops, sixty-five mosques, sixty schools, the valuable heritage library and most of the government offices. The American forces destroyed one of the two bridges in the city, both train stations, the two electricity stations, and three water-treatment plants. They also blew up the whole sanitation system and the communication network; the septic tanks contain blood and no one can communicate to anyone outside the city. Several thousand Iraqis lost their lives in the attacks.

Fallujah is now estimated to be 70 per cent bombed to the ground, with no water and no electricity. People who want to go back into that city have to get retina scans and all ten fingers fingerprinted. People inside the city are referring to it as a big jail. The goal of the mission of besieging Fallujah as announced by the US military was to capture Zarqawi and to bring security and stability for the elections, and what's left is a situation where Fallujah is in shambles, and the resistance has spread throughout the country.

(To GENERAL) General, can you comment on the current situation in Fallujah?

US GENERAL: In the history of warfare, there has never been a more humane campaign than the one waged by coalition forces, and that goes for the operations in Fallujah. We follow the law of armed conflict and hold ourselves to a high standard of accountability. We're following American principles here. And now, with your permission Sasha, can we turn to the business of the day?

US AMBASSADOR: On Sunday, the Minister of Defense announced his appointment of the top Iraqi generals in the new Iraqi army. Iraqi officers, drawn almost entirely from the many honorable men of the former Iraqi army, already command these forces. Over 70 per cent of all the men in the Iraqi army and Iraq Civil Defense Corps served honorably in the former army. They have asked to serve their country again, and we welcome their renewed service.

SASHA: Could you name the new commander, please?

US AMBASSADOR: Sure. Major Jassim Mohammed Saleh. That's all for today. Thank you. (*Leaves.*)

SASHA: General, what do you know of the new guy?

GENERAL: We know enough.

SASHA: General, is it true that this man was a Ba'athist? A senior commander under Saddam Hussein?

GENERAL: Now then, we don't know yet if he was a level two Ba'ath Party member. We really know very little about these guys yet: we've yet to talk to them all. They introduced themselves to the Marine commanders in Fallujah last week and said they had influence in the area that might prove useful.

SASHA: So there's a very real chance that you've gone to war to depose Saddam, and after killing tens of thousands of civilians you're restoring most of the original elite to power?

GENERAL: Sasha, do not exaggerate. It is true that there is some due diligence to be done on these guys before we start using them. But on the other hand, we cannot make endless checks, as the situation does not allow time for that.

SASHA: Sir, what do you make of the Iraqi nickname for Prime Minister Allawi: 'Saddam without the moustache'?

GENERAL: Off the record? Bullshit. That is all. (*Leaves.*)

SCENE 31: RANA, responding to a question.

RANA: Why do I do this? I need to do something for my people. They are the people suffering instead of the whole world, they are the people suffering from the American Empire, they are the people suffering instead of you, fighting instead of you. So whatever we can do for them is nothing compared to what they are giving.

I really believe the work I'm doing, and I have to do it, I have to help. Everybody should help. This is why you have hands, not to look at them, but to help, and if we don't help each other it will be a mess in this world. So it's my duty to help any person who is in need in this world, not only in Iraq. I've got some crazy beliefs about this, and you'll laugh of course if I tell you, but I believe that – all the time in my mind – when I'm doing this work, if I'm going to get one family out, or one person, even if I lose my life I won't lose anything because I have already saved the life of one person – I know! I knew you'd laugh! It's crazy! And if I evacuate and save the lives of two people, and lose my own life then I'm the winner, 'cos I already saved two lives.

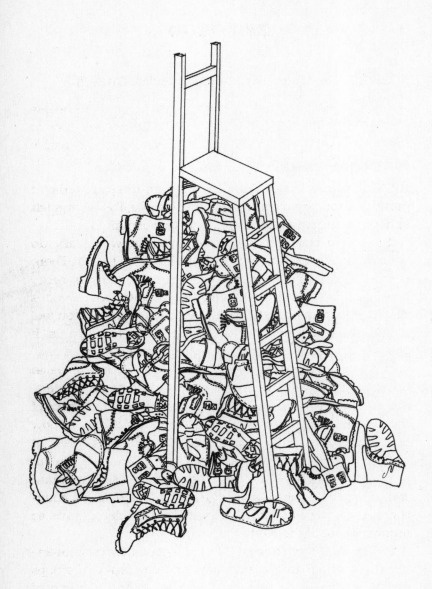

EPILOGUE

SCENE 32: A Midwestern Presbyterian Church.

A slow fade-up. The sound of prayerbooks rustling and people shifting on pews. CONDOLEEZZA RICE enters and goes to the podium, now a pulpit. This final scene should be simple and spare, no frills. Only RICE should be on stage.

RICE: Thank you for asking me up here to speak today. I grew up attending a church just like this one; I've always felt at home in the safety and sanctity of this community.

We live in troubling times, but, you know, I really do believe that God will never let his children fall too far. There is an old gospel hymn, 'He knows how much you can bear.' I really do believe that. I greatly appreciate, and so does the President, the prayers of the American people. You feel them. You know that they are there. They speak to us. If you just keep praying for us, it is so important to all of us.

In many ways, it's a wonderful White House to be in because there are a lot of people who are of faith, starting with the President. When you are in a community of the faithful, it makes a very big difference not only in how people treat each other but in how they treat the task at hand. Among American leadership, there are an awful lot of people who travel in faith. It's a remarkable thing and I think it probably sets us apart from most developed countries, where it is not something that is appreciated quite as much in most of the world.

Today, on bended knee, I thank the good Lord for protecting those of our troops overseas, and our coalition troops and innocent Iraqis who suffer at the hands of some of these senseless killings by people who are trying to shake our will.

Anyway, that's all I feel I should say here. Thank you for listening. God bless you all, and God bless America.

END.

Bankrolling Basra

by Andrew Alderson

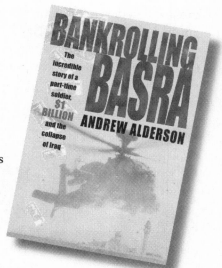

'Does anyone here know anything about finance?'

Andrew Alderson gave up his high-flying City job, looking for a new direction in life.

A member of the Territorial Army, he was called up to serve in Iraq. When he arrived in Basra he was asked if he knew 'anything about finance'. When he said yes, he got far more than he bargained for …

He was put in charge of sorting out Basra's Central Bank and told to run a multi-million dollar economy, with jurisdiction over a fifth of Iraq's finances.

But Andrew was never quite on Baghdad's radar. While the authorities were working to establish Western-style democracy he was acting as a one-man bank, delivering bin bags stuffed with millions of dollars by helicopter, speedboat and Land Rover. Getting the cash moving again quickly stabilized a tense situation.

His incredible story is one of courage, determination – and humour – set against one of the crucial episodes in modern history.

£8.99

Muhajababes

by Allegra Stratton

Why young Muslims now say it's OK to be cool, sexy and devout

Two thirds of the population in the Middle East are under 25 years old. Experts predict a crisis. In the months before turning 25 herself, Allegra Stratton set out to find out for herself.

She moves with the Middle Eastern ripple of change: Iraq's first post-Saddam elections, Lebanon's Cedar Revolution, Mubarak's decision to hold multi-candidate elections and Kuwait giving women the vote. She discovers a massive video industry of airbrushed, heavily produced, scantily-clad singers hold the affections of young Arabs. Many of the fans of these semi-naked popstrels are also very devout. 'Muhajabah' means one who veils. These, then, are the Muhajababes.

All of the young Arabs Allegra meets talk of the same Islamic revival. But though it's dressed up as trendy Islam, is it still religious conservatism? When Allegra returns, she discovers the answer may lie closer to home than she thought.

'Bold, pacy and constantly surprising.'
Sunday Times

'Direct, energetic and unpretentious.'
Guardian

£7.99

The Sleeping Buddha

by Hamida Ghafour

**The story of one family's past –
and Afghanistan's search for
a future**

Hamida Ghafour and her
family fled Kabul in 1981 when
the Russians invaded. In this
compelling memoir, she tells
how she went back in 2003
as a journalist to cover the country's
reconstruction post-9/11.

The members of Hamida's family are brought vividly to life
for us – her great-grandfather the Sufi mystic, her poetess
grandmother who urged women to unveil, her great-uncle
who wrote the first democratic constitution, her brave cousin
Bahodine who paid for his views with his life. In her family's past
she finds the story of Afghanistan itself.

She finds the country's future in people like the Midwest-
ern beautician teaching women a new kind of independence,
her cousin the parliamentary candidate and the archaeologist
digging for his country's lost civilization in the form of a giant
Sleeping Buddha.

£8.99